Essential Life Skills for Teens & Young Adults

A Practical Guide to Time & Money Management, Basics of Cooking, Cleaning, and More, So You Can Set Yourself Up for Success During & After High School

Trudy C. Marsh

Contents

Introduction

Let me guess: Picking up this book wasn't exactly your idea. Maybe your parents handed it to you, or perhaps a teacher suggested it... Either way, I'm glad you're here.

A lot of the stuff we're going to cover in this book may be old news to some of you. But other topics? They might seem like they're light-years away from your current reality. That's okay, too. Think of this as your exclusive **"preview of coming attractions"** — a sneak peek into things you'll probably have to figure out sooner than you think.

First things first: You don't need to read this book cover to cover like a novel. **Feel free to jump around** to the chapters or sections that catch your eye or seem immediately useful. Need some tips on managing your time or making a good impression with your first job? Go straight to those parts. Wondering how to handle money or what to think about when choosing a college? Those sections are there for you, too. **Use this book as your personal reference guide**, something to come back to whenever you need it.

I know, I know – you're thinking, "Why do I need a book when I can just ask my phone?" In an age where Google, YouTube, and AI tools like ChatGPT are at your fingertips, it might seem unnecessary. Yeah, of course, you can find out just about anything online. But here's the thing: Sometimes, **you don't know *what* you don't know**. And that's where this book comes in. It's like a roadmap flagging the key points of interest you'll want to explore in more detail.

This book isn't going to give you the answer to everything – that would be impossible. But it's going to provide a **comprehensive**

"shopping list" of things you should be aware of as you transition from teenage years to adulthood. It will give you a starting point for your own journey of discovery. Once something piques your interest, by all means, *PLEASE* **go on YouTube, ask ChatGPT, or simply Google** for the most recent insights, trends, and information.

As you move through the chapters, you might find some topics more relevant than others at different times in your life. That's perfectly expected. Life doesn't follow a strict sequence, and neither should your learning. This book isn't a cover-to-cover read; **treat it like a reference book**. Jump around. Use the bits you need, *when* you need them.

This isn't a once-and-done read, either—it's your companion for years to come. Maybe right now, you want to learn how to manage your money or understand the basics of cooking. In a few years, you might come back to delve into the sections on filing tax returns or home maintenance. Grow into these skills at your own pace, so when the time comes, you'll be ready. By flipping through these pages, you're not jumping the gun—you're **getting ahead of the game**.

This book is just a guide. Your journey is uniquely yours, and you'll learn a lot by living it, making mistakes, and finding your own path. Use this book as a compass to point you in the right direction, to ask the right questions, and to help you build a foundation of skills that you can continue to expand upon as you grow.

So, whether you picked up this book out of curiosity, necessity, or because someone thought it was a good idea for you, welcome! You're at the start of an exciting path – full of challenges, surprises, and opportunities. Equip yourself with knowledge, stay curious, and keep an open mind. The world is waiting for you to make your mark, and this book is here to help you get started.

Chapter One

The Body Basics

Taking Care of Your Physical Self

I n the grand game of life, it often feels like someone else holds all the cards. As a teenager, you rely on your parents for many things, are bound by their rules, and may not be free to make as many decisions as you would like.

But there's one deck you've got a firm grip on: Your physical health. Your body is the one thing that's truly yours, the vehicle that carries you through every experience. While there are many things you might not get to choose, you have the power to decide how to fuel, maintain, and drive this incredible machine. By taking care of your body, you're not just feeling good—you're taking back some control.

EAT: Choices That Count

Think of food as your body's power source – it's what keeps your mind sharp and your energy up and gives your skin that healthy glow. Food is about more than just satisfying your taste buds. When you nourish yourself with the right nutrients, you're fueling your body to perform at its peak.

"A Balanced Diet" — you hear that a lot, but what is it, exactly? Well, it's actually simple. A balanced diet is all about *variety*.

- *Fruits and Vegetables:* These are nature's multivitamins. They're packed with vitamins, minerals, and fiber. Aim for a rainbow of colors to get a wide range of nutrients.

- **Proteins:** Think of these as your body's building blocks. They help to build and repair tissues. Good sources include lean meats, poultry, fish, beans, eggs, and nuts.

- **Grains:** Preferably whole grains. They provide energy and are a good source of fiber, which helps with digestion.

- **Dairy:** These products are a great source of calcium, which is essential for strong bones and teeth.

- **Fats:** Yes, you read that right. Fats are an essential part of a balanced diet. They provide energy and help your body absorb specific vitamins. Be sure to choose healthy fats, like those found in avocados, nuts, seeds, and olive oil.

- **Water:** Last but not least, staying hydrated is essential for your bodily functions to work correctly. Dehydration can be dangerous, so keep water handy all day and sip regularly.

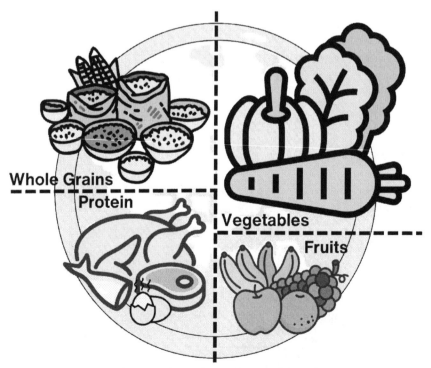

Rough Visual Guide to the Healthy Plate

Simple Ways to Eat Healthier

- **Make It Easy:** If healthy eating is convenient, you're more likely to stick to it. Think about foods that are low-prep and easily portable. Fruit, small bags of nuts, seeds, trail mix, granola bars, single-serve yogurts, or veggie sticks with dip can make quick, nutritious snacks.

- **Swap or Add:** Love your large Frappuccino? Consider ordering a smaller size, switching to skim milk, or choosing sugar-free syrup. You can also balance a sweet drink with a small salad, fruit, or protein option like egg bites.

- **Make It a Habit:** Try to eat meals at the same time every day to reduce the risk of skipping them, which can result in low blood sugar, tiredness, or sugar cravings.

MOVE: Energize Every Day

Your body is designed to move and loves it! Regular physical activity makes you stronger and also boosts your mental well-being. The goal? A minimum of 60 minutes of moderate-to-vigorous exercise every day. Yep, EVERY DAY!

There are four essential types of physical activity:

Aerobic/Cardiovascular Activity: These activities help your heart and lungs work better, can lift your mood, and make you feel more energetic. Plus, they're great for staying in shape and keeping your mind sharp! Think running, biking, swimming, dancing, or team sports. Do these daily.

Muscle Strengthening: Exercises like weightlifting, resistance bands, bodyweight exercises, or chores like shoveling snow help build muscle strength and endurance. Do these three times a week.

Bone Strengthening: Your bones need exercise to avoid becoming brittle and weak. Activities that involve some sort of impact, like running or jumping, help increase bone density and keep bones strong. Three times a week is the goal.

Flexibility Training: Stretching helps to improve your flexibility, allowing your joints to move through their full range of motion. It also helps to prevent injuries and relieve muscle tension. Simple stretching exercises, yoga, or Pilates are great ways to improve flexibility. Do this whenever you can throughout the day.

Take the stairs instead of the elevator, bike or skate to school, and help with backyard chores. Every bit counts! It's all about finding what works for you and making it a part of your lifestyle.

SLEEP: Your Body's Reset Button

Sleep is a process that allows your body and brain to rest, heal, and repair, but teenagers tend not to get enough of it. Aiming for **8 to 10 hours a night** isn't just a recommendation; it's a necessity. This nightly ritual doesn't just offer rest; it's a vital tune-up for every tissue and system, ensuring they are primed and ready for the challenges ahead.

Building Good Sleep Habits

- **Make Your Bedroom Sleep-Friendly:** Your bedroom should be a place of relaxation — comfortable, slightly cooler, and free of distractions. Make it as dark as possible at night to signal your brain that it's time to sleep. A "white noise" machine may help if you are sensitive to sounds.

- **Turn Technology Off:** The blue light emitted by smartphones and tablets over-stimulates your brain and messes with your body's internal clock, making it harder to fall asleep. Turn off screens at least an hour before bed. Put devices in "do not disturb" mode during the overnight hours.

- **Maintain a Consistent Sleep Schedule:** Try to go to bed and wake up at the same time every day, even on weekends. The closer you can match your sleep and wake times daily, the easier it will be to fall asleep and wake up feeling refreshed.

- **Practice Calming Activities Before Bed:** Chances are, your parents had a bedtime routine for you when you were little. Set up a new routine for yourself: Meditation, bedtime yoga, journaling, or reading a relaxing book can help signal to your body that it's time to wind down and fall asleep.

- **Allocate Adequate Time for Sleep:** It can be challenging to get a full night's sleep with all the pressures you face as a teenager. How many hours of sleep do you currently average per night? Find out, then increase it by 30 minutes a week until you reach the recommended 8-10 hours a night.

Taking care of your physical self doesn't stop at meeting the bare minimum of what it takes to stay alive. Skincare and basic medical care are also essential for maintaining good health and presenting the best version of yourself to the world.

SKIN AND ACNE CARE

Dealing with acne can be frustrating, but the right skincare regimen can make a difference. Hormonal changes can ramp up oil production, leading to clogged pores when this oil combines with dead skin cells and bacteria. This results in pimples, blackheads, and whiteheads. Genetics, diet, and lifestyle factors can also play a big role. Your skincare routine should include:

Cleansing: Use a gentle cleanser. Harsh cleansers and hot water can strip your skin of essential oils, triggering even more oil production. So use cool to tepid water to wash your face twice daily — in the morning and before bedtime.

Moisturizing: Use a fragrance-free moisturizer to avoid an allergic reaction or skin irritation. Apply one with an SPF in the morning; apply a night moisturizer without sunscreen before bed.

Acne Meds: It might be tempting, but don't squeeze or pop pimples. Use an acne spot treatment specifically designed to safely dry the pimple without damaging the skin.

Toning and Exfoliating: Toners are an optional skincare step. You apply them to the face using a cotton pad to remove any excess oil or dirt left behind after washing. Exfoliating the skin is also optional and must be done with care. Exfoliate no more than once a week, or you might irritate the skin.

COMMON/MINOR MEDICAL ISSUES

No matter how careful you are, you will fall sick from time to time as long as you live. Some common illnesses include:

- **The Common Cold:** Symptoms can include a sore throat, a headache, a runny or stuffy nose, cough, sneezing, fatigue, and mild fever.

- **Influenza, a.k.a. Flu:** The symptoms of flu are similar to the common cold but are more severe. High fever, strong chills, intense body aches, sometimes with diarrhea or vomiting.

- **Infections:** Caused by various microorganisms such as bacteria, viruses, fungi, and parasites. Fever, aches, and other flu-like symptoms are common, but these are often accompanied by discomfort or swelling of the particular parts of the body that are affected, e.g., ears, sinuses, and urinary tracts.

The key is to listen to your body, notice when something feels off, and take appropriate measures.

Now, I am not a medical professional, so I can't give you medical advice, but let me just share some commonly and generally accepted ways of dealing with minor illnesses and injuries here.

Over-the-Counter Medications

All right, so you've identified your symptoms. Now what? *Over-the-counter (OTC)* medications can help you feel better for some common illnesses. OTC means that you can buy them at the pharmacy without a doctor's prescription.

Nonsteroidal anti-inflammatory drugs (NSAIDs) like ibuprofen can be helpful for pain, fever, or inflammation. *Antihistamines* might be your best friend if you're dealing with a runny nose, sneezing, itching, or watery eyes. Got a cough? *Cough suppressants* can help.

OTC means you can buy them without a doctor's note, but that doesn't mean they're harmless. Before you buy anything, consult the pharmacist at the drugstore. Always read the label, follow the directions, and be aware of potential side effects.

COMMON AND SEASONAL ALLERGIES

If you have ever woken up with red, swollen eyes, broken out in a rash after eating something, or had sneezing fits you couldn't control, you have probably experienced an allergic reaction. Allergies happen when the body's immune system overreacts to something it considers harmful, like certain foods, animals, dust, or pollen.

Handling Common Allergies

Food Allergies: Some people are born with it, but you can develop food allergies anytime, even with foods you've been eating all your life. Food allergies can be severe – sometimes even deadly. If you have allergies, ask staff at restaurants about ingredients and always tell them if you have any allergies. Carry an *epinephrine auto-injector* (like an *EpiPen*) and know how to use it. Let your companions know that you carry one and show them where to find it. Carry an allergen card with information on your allergy and how to treat it in case of emergency.

Contact Allergies: Contact allergies happen after touching a substance that sets off an immune response, like latex, certain metals, or chemicals. Sometimes, the source is obvious, but other times, patch testing by an allergist is necessary to identify your allergen. Choose hypoallergenic cosmetics and skincare products less likely to cause skin reactions, and choose fragrance-free products.

Seasonal Allergies (Hay Fever): Pollen is a common source of seasonal allergies. Spring and fall can be challenging for hay fever sufferers, whose symptoms include itchy eyes, sinus headaches, non-stop runny nose, and constant sneezing. Close windows on high pollen days, and wear a mask outdoors. Using *nasal irrigation devices* (like *Neti Pot*) to rinse out your nasal passages can feel a bit weird at first, but it really works for some people.

Sinus Irrigation Devices

Antihistamines can provide relief from hay fever symptoms. There are day and night formulations. **Decongestants**, either in nasal spray or oral form, can help with congestion. Eye drops and topical **corticosteroids** can relieve eye and skin symptoms. While over-the-counter solutions might give you temporary relief, it's important to consult a healthcare expert for advice about side effects and your specific allergies.

If your symptoms are severe, last for more than a few days, or if OTC medications aren't helping, it's time to call your doctor. Also, if you have symptoms like chest pain, difficulty breathing, severe abdominal pain, sudden dizziness, or severe vomiting or diarrhea, seek medical help right away.

BASIC FIRST AID

Not every minor illness or injury warrants a doctor's visit. Having a basic understanding of first aid can save you time and money. Here's a quick guide to generally recommended popular treatments of everyday first aid emergencies.

- **Cuts, Scratches, and Scrapes:** Clean the wound with mild soap and water and apply an *antibiotic ointment* to prevent infection. Cover with a sterile bandage or dressing.

- **Minor Burns:** Run cold water over the burn for a few minutes, then gently pat dry with a clean cloth. Apply an antibiotic ointment to soothe the skin and cover the burn with a sterile, non-stick dressing.

- **Bug Bites & Poison Ivy:** Wash with soap and water and apply an over-the-counter *hydrocortisone cream* or *calamine lotion* to relieve itching and inflammation. Take an antihistamine if recommended by a healthcare professional. If you are allergic to bees and get stung, seek help right away.

- **Splinters:** Clean the area around the splinter with soap and water. Use sterilized tweezers to remove the splinter gently. Apply an antibiotic ointment.

- **Nosebleeds:** Tilt your head forward slightly, pinch your nostrils together, and breathe through your mouth. Maintain pressure until the bleeding stops.

- **Sunburn:** Take a cool bath or shower to soothe the skin. Apply aloe vera gel to hydrate and calm the skin. Avoid further sun exposure until your skin has healed.

- **Panic Attacks:** Focus on slow, deep breaths to regulate your breathing pattern. Find a quiet and comfortable place to sit or lie down. Practice grounding techniques, such as naming objects around you.

- **Hyperventilation:** Hyperventilating can be confusing—you feel short of air because you are breathing out too much carbon dioxide too quickly, NOT because you're not getting enough oxygen. Breathing in and out of a paper bag or cupped hands can help, for the time being, by increasing your CO_2 intake, but exercise caution and ask your doctor for advice.

- **Concussions:** Call a doctor if you hit your head hard and suspect a concussion. Rest in a quiet, dark room and avoid activities that require concentration or physical exertion until symptoms subside.

- **Sports Injuries:** For sprained wrists and ankles, jabbed fingers, and hyper-extended joints, follow the R.I.C.E method: **Rest** the injured area to prevent further damage, apply an **Ice** pack wrapped in a cloth to reduce swelling and pain, use an elastic bandage to **Compress** the injured area for support and reduce swelling, and **Elevate** the injured area above heart level whenever possible.

- **Broken Bones:** If you think you may have broken a bone, go to the hospital emergency room, call 911, or contact a doctor. They will take an x-ray and give you proper treatment and instructions.

- **Severe Allergic Reaction:** If an allergic reaction is severe, call 911. If the affected person uses an EpiPen, follow the instructions on the pen to administer it.

- **Ingestion or Exposure to Harmful Chemicals.** Call the Poison Control Center: **1-800-222-1222.**

- **Choking:** If the person can cough or speak, encourage them to continue coughing. If they can't breathe, perform the *Heimlich Maneuver*. If you're not confident performing the Heimlich, get help or call 911 immediately.

Again, it is called '*First* Aid' for a reason. These are just the immediate and often temporary fixes for common injuries. If your condition doesn't improve or gets worse, be sure to seek professional help.

The Basic First Aid Kit

The following is a list of items you should consider including in your home first aid kit or your medicine cabinet:

Adhesive Bandages (i.e., Bandaid)	Various sizes for minor cuts, blisters, or abrasions.
Sterile Gauze Pads	Different sizes to help cover more significant wounds or burns.
Adhesive Tape	To hold gauze and other dressings in place.
Antiseptic Wipes or Solution	For cleaning wounds. Examples include hydrogen peroxide or alcohol wipes.
Tweezers	For removing splinters or other foreign objects.
Scissors	For cutting tape, gauze, or clothing.
Thermometer	To check for fever.
Elastic Bandage (e.g., Ace bandage)	For wrapping sprains or strains.
Pain Relievers	Such as acetaminophen (Tylenol) or ibuprofen (Advil). Always follow the recommended dosages and keep out of reach of children.
Antihistamine	Like diphenhydramine (Benadryl) for allergic reactions. Be aware it can cause drowsiness.
Hydrocortisone Cream	For insect bites or itchy rashes.
Burn Cream or Aloe Vera Gel	To soothe minor burns.
List of Emergency Numbers	Including contacts for your family doctor and local emergency services. If you suspect ingestion or exposure to harmful chemicals, contact the Poison Control Center at 1-800-222-1222.

Basic CPR

Cardiopulmonary resuscitation, or *CPR*, is a lifesaving technique used in emergencies like a heart attack or near-drowning. It's a bit too complex to cover here, so take a CPR course as soon as you have an opportunity to learn the correct method. It can really save lives.

Remember, the aim of first aid isn't to replace professional medical help. It's to provide immediate assistance until that help arrives. And while it's great to be prepared, here's hoping you'll never have to use these skills!

In health matters, it's always better to play it safe. If something feels wrong, listen to your gut and seek help. You've only got one body. Take good care of it.

Chapter Two

Medical Matters

Staying Informed, Staying Healthy

E ven with the best self-care routines, including a balanced diet, regular exercise, and ample sleep, we all need professional medical care from time to time. Routine check-ups help ensure our bodies are running smoothly, and let's face it, illnesses and injuries are a part of life no one can fully evade.

REGULAR CHECK-UPS: Your Body's Report Card

Medical Check-Ups

At a typical check-up or health screening, your doctor takes a survey of your overall health. They'll listen to your heart and lungs, take your blood pressure, and examine various parts of your body for unusual signs.

Blood tests are another regular feature. These can give a detailed report about your cholesterol levels, blood sugar, kidney function, etc. A good rule of thumb is to have a general check-up once a year.

Areas of Concern

Cholesterol: It's not just for old folks. Approximately 7% of American children and adolescents have high cholesterol levels, which can lead to an increased risk of heart disease or stroke.

Blood pressure: Around 3.5% of children and teens in the United States have high blood pressure. That number jumps to almost 50% of adults over 20. Small lifestyle changes in your adolescent years can help you avoid big problems later.

Body Mass: Maintaining a healthy weight is a way to lower your risk of multiple chronic conditions. Adults use a standard *Body Mass Index (BMI)* calculation to see whether their weight falls within a healthy range for their height. Children and teens use a gender-and-age-based BMI calculation, best managed by a doctor.

Blood Sugar Level: Chronically high blood sugar can contribute to developing *Type 2 Diabetes*, a rising condition in children and teens.

Smoking: Smoking harms your heart, lungs, and overall health. If you smoke, **QUIT!!** There is no benefit to it. If you are having a difficult time quitting, reach out to medical professionals.

Dental Check-Ups

Your dentist will thoroughly clean your teeth and gums, check for cavities, and take X-rays if needed. Ideally, schedule a visit every six months. An *orthodontist* is a dental specialist specializing in teeth alignment and jaw function, ensuring that you have a healthy bite.

Dental Care Tips

- Brush your teeth at least twice daily, once when you wake up and once before bed. Floss first to dislodge any food particles or plaque between teeth, which makes brushing more effective. It should take at least a full minute to brush your upper and lower teeth and the teeth at the back.

- Replace your toothbrush every three to four months.

- Don't hesitate to make a dental appointment if you develop a toothache, swollen or bleeding gums, or suffer an injury to your teeth, such as a cracked or chipped tooth.

Eye Examinations

Regular eye exams can detect eye conditions like glaucoma and cataracts and even spot signs of other health issues like diabetes or high blood pressure. During an eye exam, your eye doctor will check your vision, examine your eyes for common conditions, and possibly dilate your pupils for a more detailed look. A standard recommendation is an exam every two years. If you wear glasses or contact lenses or have an eye condition, you might need to visit your *optometrist* more often.

VACCINATIONS

Vaccinations prepare your immune system to fight off infections before they invade your body. They protect you against various diseases, from measles and mumps to influenza and *HPV (Human Papillomavirus)*. They're not just for kids, either. Teens and adults need vaccinations, too, including boosters for certain vaccines.

Flu viruses mutate constantly, so last year's flu shot will not protect you against this year's virus. So, you should get a flu shot every fall to be safe. The same applies to COVID-19 vaccines, as they are constantly evolving along with the virus.

Your doctor can provide a vaccination schedule based on age, health, and previous vaccination history. Keep your vaccinations up to date. It's crucial for your health and those around you.

MEDICAL CARE

Nobody knows more about your changing body than you, so it makes sense that you start taking your medical care into your own hands. Prepare for that responsibility now, starting with the following:

- *Gather basic information:* Name and address of your doctor, copies of your health records, names of medications you take, and family health history.

- *Choose your own doctor:* Talk to your parents about transitioning from a pediatrician or family doctor, and research who you might want as your own doctor. Of course, you can keep your current doctor if you like them!

* **Do it yourself:** Start making appointments and calling in your own prescriptions.

* **Learn how things are done:** Start learning about insurance coverage basics and getting your own once you are no longer under your parent's plan. Ask them how referrals to specialists are made and any other process you don't completely understand.

Different Types of Doctors

Not all doctors are the same. There are many areas of specialization. Some doctors are available for anyone to visit, while others require a referral from your *primary care* (i.e., main) doctor to make an appointment.

Here are some of the most common types of doctors you are likely to need:

* **Pediatrician:** They specialize in care for children from birth to young adulthood, usually age 18.

* **Family Doctor:** Sometimes referred to as general practitioners or internists, these doctors care for the whole family, from birth to old age. They manage routine checkups, some chronic illness care, and give vaccinations.

* **Dermatologist:** This is who you see if you have a problem with your skin, hair, or nails, such as acne, eczema, or moles.

* **Optometrist & Ophthalmologist:** Either can be referred to as "eye doctor," but there is an important distinction. *Optometrists* specialize in correcting your vision with glasses and contact lenses. *Ophthalmologists* treat eye conditions and diseases and also perform eye surgery.

- **OBGYN or Gynecologist:** OBGYN is short for *Doctor of Obstetrics and Gynecology*. These doctors specialize in the female reproductive system, pregnancy, and childbirth. Often, young women are encouraged to start seeing gynecologists during high school.

This is just the tip of the iceberg! A family physician or pediatrician can guide you should you need to see a specialist for anything. Rely on their expertise.

Health Insurance

While you might feel invincible now, life has unpredictable moments, and having health insurance can make a world of difference, especially when something bad happens. But it's not just for emergencies; it's also for regular check-ups, preventive care, and peace of mind.

Regardless of which doctor you need to see, you will need your health insurance card.

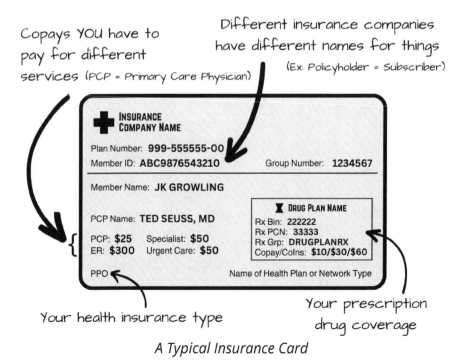

A Typical Insurance Card

There are many different kinds of health insurance plans, so it's a good idea to get familiar with them now before you are responsible for finding your own. Ask your parents what type of insurance they have for you, and talk about your options for when you are no longer covered under their plan. Understanding how health insurance works can be complicated, but knowing key terms can help simplify things.

Types of Health Insurance

There's quite a range of health insurance types out there, but here are the most common ones:

- **Health Maintenance Organizations (HMOs):** One of the most affordable types of health insurance, but also one of the least flexible. These plans limit coverage to doctors who work for or with the HMO. It generally won't cover out-of-network care except in an emergency. An HMO may require you to live or work in its service area to be eligible for coverage.

- **Preferred Provider Organizations (PPOs):** This plan offers the most freedom but typically has the highest premiums. These plans contract with medical providers, such as hospitals and doctors, to create a *network of participating providers*. You pay less if you use providers in the plan's network. You can use doctors, hospitals, and providers outside the network for additional costs.

- **Exclusive Provider Organizations (EPOs):** These are much like PPOs but might not cover care outside their network except in emergencies.

Understanding Health Insurance Terms

Health insurance comes with its own language. Once you understand it, things get a lot less confusing. Here are some key terms:

Premium: This is the monthly cost you pay for having health insurance, <u>whether you use it or not.</u>

Co-Pay: A co-pay is a specific amount you will pay each time you have a medical expense, and the insurance company pays the rest of the bill for that medical service.

Deductible: This is the amount you must pay out-of-pocket for covered health services within a year before your insurance company begins to cover expenses. For example, if your policy has a $2,000 deductible, you'll be responsible for the first $2,000 of your covered medical costs each year. After that, your insurance company will start contributing based on the terms of your policy.

Out-of-Pocket Maximum: This is the most you'll pay annually for covered services. Once you hit this limit, your insurance will pay 100% for covered benefits.

Reimbursement: Some insurance companies require you to pay for services first, and then they will pay you back after you submit a *claim*.

Group ID, Member ID, Policyholder: The Group ID number identifies the employer plan you are insured under. The Member ID identifies you. The Policyholder is the person who holds the policy – like your parents.

Provider: Refers to medical service providers, i.e., doctors, hospitals, clinics, x-ray technicians, testing labs, etc.

Primary Care Physician (PCP): This is your main doctor, who must refer you to a specialist. A *specialist* is an expert in one specific field of medicine, such as a dermatologist or ophthalmologist.

Referrals and Pre-Authorizations: When you need to see a specialist, you almost always need your primary care physician to write a referral for you. A pre-authorization is when the insurance company has to approve a treatment before they will pay for it.

Prescription: A note written by a doctor that authorizes a patient to receive medication or treatment. You take it to your pharmacy (or "call it in") to have it "filled."

Explanation of Benefits (EOB): This is a statement your insurance company mails out that shows what treatments or services you received, the amounts billed by the provider, how much insurance did or did not cover, and how much you are responsible for. These should be kept on file in case they must be presented later.

| INSURANCE COMPANY NAME | **Explanation of Benefits** |
| | **This Is Not a Bill** |

Patient Name: JK GROWLING
Place of Service: Outpatient
Date Received: 10/31/2024

Member ID: ABC9876543210
Group Number: 1234567

Claim Number: XX888888888888
Type of Service: Medical
Date Processed: 11/30/2024

Provider: Hogsmeld Hospital
Provider ID: HP1234567

					Patient Responsibility			
Date of Service	Description of Service	Amount Billed	Other Insurance Paid	Your Plan Paid	Deductible	Co-Insurance	Co-Pay	Amount You Owe
10/31/2024	Emergency	$$$$$$$$	$0	$$$$$$$$	$$$	$$$	$$$	$$$
10/31/2024	X-ray	$$$$$$$$	$0	$$$$$$$$	$$$	$$$	$$$	$$$
Claim Total		$$$$$$$$	$0	$$$$$$$$	$$$	$$$	$$$	$$$

An Example of EOB

In Network vs. Out of Network: Insurance companies often have contracts with certain providers in your area, who will offer you discounted rates for their services. They are called *in-network providers*. Choosing a provider who is not on that list means you will have to pay the full price. These are called *out-of-network providers*. Try not to use out-of-network providers unless you have to. It can be VERY expensive.

Importance of Health Insurance

Let's just get one thing straight: **You MUST have health Insurance**.

Without health insurance, every visit to the doctor, accidental fall, or serious illness will cost you full price to get treated. Medication, therapy, or medical expenses such as hospital stays can add up *very* quickly.

If your parents don't have or can't afford health insurance, you still have options:

1. **Medicaid:** This state and federal program provides health coverage if you have a very low income. The maximum age you can be covered and the services provided can vary by state.

2. **CHIP (Children's Health Insurance Program):** This program is designed for families who may earn too much to qualify for Medicaid but still can't afford private insurance. It covers children up to age 19.

3. **Catastrophic Health Insurance:** You might qualify for this if you're under 30. It's a type of health insurance with lower monthly premiums but a high deductible, designed to cover worst-case scenarios.

4. **School Insurance:** Some colleges offer low-cost health insurance to students. If you're heading to or already in college, check to see if this is an option.

5. **Local Health Departments or Clinics:** They often offer free or low-cost medical care. They might also be aware of local health programs that can assist you.

6. **Part-time Job with Benefits:** Some employers provide health insurance benefits even for part-time positions.

Health insurance isn't just for treating medical problems after something happens. It is also for prevention. Without insurance, all those check-ups we talked about earlier may be unaffordable.

Speaking of prevention...

LET'S TALK ABOUT SEX!

Don't panic! This is not a section on the reproductive system or the mechanics of sex. It's a section on how to approach sex and the potential consequences of sexual activity from a no-nonsense, mature perspective.

Abstinence

Many people choose not to engage in sexual activity for various reasons. Sex changes a relationship, sometimes for the better and sometimes for the worse. Sharing your body with another person is very intimate, and not everyone is ready for that at a young age. Some people choose to abstain for religious or cultural reasons. Others simply because they just aren't ready or don't want to.

You don't need to justify your decision to anyone. Your body is yours alone, and you control what you do with it. Open, honest conversations with your partner about your expectations are vital to avoid misunderstandings. Your partner should never pressure you into doing something you are uncomfortable with.

If you are going to have sex

The decision to have sex is a seriously big step which should not be taken lightly. Your age, your partner's age, your family's views, your culture, religion... the list of factors that come into play goes on and on. Ideally, you should discuss it with a trusted adult. And if you have any doubts at all about it, it's probably a sign that it's not your time yet. Don't rush into it. You have plenty of time!

But if you are determined to go ahead, **this book can't stop you**; so it may as well arm you with information you can use to protect yourself. It is absolutely essential that you know how to avoid *sexually transmitted diseases (STDs)* or *sexually transmitted infections (STIs)* and understand how birth control works to prevent unwanted pregnancies. Knowledge is power, and both males and females should be well-informed before taking that big step.

Before you do anything...

- **Birth control** *is a* **non-negotiable:** Birth control, or *contraceptives*, is the responsibility of *both* partners and should not fall on just one. Discussing sexual history, what type of protection to use, and who will be responsible for getting the protective device — are the essential, non-sexy aspects of a mature sexual relationship. You should also talk about what will happen if pregnancy results.

- **Testing:** Getting tested for STIs before engaging in sex is crucial. A caring partner will want to ensure that both of you are protected. Some diseases, such as HPV, can be transmitted non-sexually, so you can be infected without ever having sex. Knowing your status and that of your partner before becoming intimate is essential.

STDs and STIs

The terminology may change from *STDs (sexually transmitted diseases)* to *STIs (sexually transmitted infections)*, but the basics remain the same. Sex can bring unwanted consequences in the form of illness and infection. STIs are spread from partner to partner through sexual contact. If you are having sex and are concerned that you may have been exposed to STIs, don't hesitate. Make an appointment with a doctor and get tested. Many are treatable, and you can avoid long-lasting consequences if they're caught and treated early.

Half of STDs and STIs in the United States are diagnosed in people between the ages of 15 and 24. You don't have to "sleep around" to be at risk, either; all it takes is one exposure. Take the following precautions to reduce your risk.

- **Abstinence:** This is the only way to avoid STIs completely.

- **Protection:** Condoms are a form of birth control, but are also the only contraceptive that protects you from STIs. We will cover different types of contraceptives in detail in the next section.

- **Get tested:** Get tested before having sex with a partner for the first time, and then get tested regularly once having intercourse. Being monogamous with one person can reduce the risk, but if you or your partner engages in sex outside the relationship, it can put the other partner at risk.

- **Health Checkups:** Testing is part of sexual health, but so are regular sexual health checkups covering both the physical and emotional side of your sex life. Suppose you are having sex but feeling uncomfortable, afraid, sad, or concerned in any way. In that case, a sexual health professional can help you uncover what is really going on. Start with a conversation with your family doctor.

Contraceptives (i.e., Birth Control)

Important! Many birth control methods are effective at preventing pregnancy, but ALL should be used with condoms to protect against STDs and STIs. Be sure to consult your doctor to determine the best method for your situation.

Condoms, a.k.a. "Rubber": Male condoms are worn on the penis by males during intercourse. Female condoms are inserted inside the vagina ahead of time. These are the only things that protect you against BOTH pregnancy *and* STIs.

Contraceptive Implants: This is a small device implanted into the skin of the upper arm of females. It contains a *progestin hormone* that stops the ovary from releasing eggs. It lasts three to five years before it needs to be replaced.

IUDs: A small device, with or without a hormone, inserted by a healthcare provider into the uterus of a female. Depending on the type, it does not have to be replaced for many years and can make menstrual periods lighter.

Hormonal Contraceptives: These can come in various forms, including a patch, pill, or ring. They have the added benefit of making your period lighter and more regular.

Progestin Injection: An injection that prevents ovaries from releasing eggs for three months. Requires a visit to a healthcare provider for a shot every three months. May cause weight gain and affect bone density if used for long periods.

Contraceptive Vaginal Ring or Patch: The estrogen and progestin ring is inserted into the vagina to prevent the ovaries from releasing an egg. It remains in place for three weeks and then is removed for a week to allow for a menstrual period. The patch works similarly but is placed on the skin, not in the vagina.

Gels and Spermicides: A gel or cream that makes it difficult for sperm to swim, offering some protection against pregnancy. It should be used with other birth control devices described above, *not* by itself.

It is important to remember that, even after taking precautions, none of these methods – except abstinence – is 100% effective 100% of the time. So, females need to pay close attention to their bodies after having sex for any signs of change.

Pregnancy

If you engage in sexual intercourse without protection, a condom broke, or you have reasons to believe that your chosen method of birth control has failed, in some states, "the morning-after pill," which prevents a fertilized egg from implanting, may be available OTC at your local pharmacy. For it to be effective, It is important to take it as soon as possible following intercourse. Note that this should NOT be used as a regular method of contraception because it is not as effective as other methods and has potential side effects. **Be sure to consult your PCP or gynecologist about this particular method of contraception AHEAD OF TIME to get reliable, professional advice and information.**

Missing a menstrual period is often the first sign of pregnancy. Other physical symptoms can take much longer to appear. If you suspect pregnancy, don't ignore it and hope it goes away. The sooner you know for sure, the more options you will have. Act immediately and get tested. Home pregnancy tests are available at your local pharmacy.

What do you do if you or your partner becomes pregnant? Depending on where you live, different options are available to you. **The first step is to talk to your parents or guardians.** They need to know this. The next step is to find an appropriate healthcare provider, i.e., a gynecologist, to help with whichever next steps you choose.

Pregnancy Options

If you or your partner get pregnant, there are basically three options for you.

Parenting: You can keep and raise the child yourselves. Getting the correct *prenatal care* (care for the pregnant person and the unborn child) is key to helping ensure a safe, healthy pregnancy and birth.

Adoption: Another option is to carry a baby to term and then put them up for adoption by another family. A healthcare provider can refer you to the appropriate resources based on where you live to get the process started.

Abortion: Depending on where you live, abortion may be an option. Ending a pregnancy can be a traumatic experience, but a healthcare provider can help you.

Facing an unplanned pregnancy can be overwhelming. The pregnant mother is being forced to make a life-changing decision that will affect her for the rest of her life, and she will need all the support she can get, regardless of her choice. Seeking counsel from healthcare experts and confiding in parents or a trusted figure will make all the difference during such a stressful time.

Medical Matters might sound serious now, but getting a handle on them early sets you up for a healthier teen life and beyond. Use what you've learned here to take charge and stay on top of your well-being.

Chapter Three

Mind Matters

Taking Care of Your Mental Self

N avigating the maze of emotions, thoughts, and feelings? You're not alone! Mental health, often treated as a hush-hush subject, is as significant as that daily workout or apple-a-day; let's have an open conversation about it, for your mental well-being deserves the same attention and care as your physical health.

First, let's clear the air about what mental health really is. Contrary to what some people might think, mental health isn't just about mental illnesses or disorders. It's much broader than that. It's about how we think, feel, and behave in general. It influences how we handle stress, relate to others, and make decisions. In other words, it's an integral part of our daily lives.

UNDERSTANDING AND MANAGING EMOTIONS

EQ (Emotional Intelligence Quotient) is like *IQ (Intelligence Quotient)* but for feelings. It is a way to assess your ability to recognize and control your own emotions and to recognize emotions in others, including the impact your behavior has on those around you.

The process of measuring your EQ is more complicated than IQ, and is actually not important. The concept of EQ is useful when you keep it in mind as a framework to evaluate how you are doing on the emotions front. There are four areas of emotional intelligence everyone should be trying to improve:

Self-Awareness: Accurately naming your emotions is the first step to controlling them. Many people think they are angry when they are actually frustrated, disappointed, or overwhelmed. Identifying complex emotions can improve your EQ and help you better understand your strengths and limitations.

Self-Management: This is self-control. We can't always control the emotions that pop up in different situations, but we can learn how to respond appropriately. You *can* control your responses.

Social Awareness: This one isn't about you but about how to become aware of the needs of others. Are you always the last to realize when someone is upset with you? Being aware of the feelings of others and showing empathy is a good way to boost your EQ.

Relationship Management: People with high EQ work on their social skills to positively impact all types of relationships. Those with strong social skills know how to manage relationships with friends, parents, siblings, teachers, coaches, or other community members. (We'll get into this more in the next chapter.)

Emotional Triggers

Emotional triggers are things like people, places, or situations that would be no big deal for other people but provoke a negative and often strong emotion in *you* because of a past experience or irrational fear.

There are three categories of triggers:

1. *Anxiety Trigger:* These can make you feel panicked, seemingly out of nowhere.

2. *Trauma Trigger:* This is when something in the present reminds you of something traumatic that happened in the past, causing you to try and avoid it.

3. *Anger Triggers:* These triggers can fill you with sudden rage that is difficult to control.

Emotional triggers vary from person to person. Common physical reactions to emotional triggers include: chest pain, rapid heart rate, shaking, dizziness, sweating, and nausea.

Coping with Emotional Triggers

When something sets you off, pause and reflect on what just happened and your reaction to it. Don't brush your feelings under the rug; instead, dig deeper to recognize patterns that reveal your triggers.

It's completely fine to experience these emotions; give yourself a breather to process them. Doing so allows you to see things more clearly and pick a better way to soothe yourself.

Struggling to pinpoint triggers or handle your reactions? Consider therapy. It's a valuable space to unpack emotions and arm you with coping tools.

PATH: A Way to Manage Emotions

The Mental Health Association has a four-step process called "PATH" to help manage emotions in a healthy way.

Pause: Learn to react slowly. Take deep breaths, count to 100, or even excuse yourself to the washroom for a few minutes before reacting.

Acknowledge: Acknowledge your feelings and that they are valid. Allow yourself to feel the emotions without feeling the need to react immediately.

Think: Think before you act so you don't do things that may be harmful out of impulse. Brainstorm some things you can do to make yourself feel better.

Help: Take action to help yourself! Consider steps from one of the following categories:

Mood Boosters	Actions that make you feel better, like watching a movie or calling a friend.
Self-Care	We often neglect our basic needs when we feel bad. Have a glass of water and a snack, take a shower, or get some rest.
Let Your Feelings Out	Letting your emotions out can be therapeutic. Write down your feelings, punch a pillow, or even cry out loud.
Problem-Solve	Brainstorm about ways to avoid feeling this way over the same thing in the future.

When Emotions Get Out of Hand

Handling emotions can be tricky. Sometimes, we might dodge them or lash out, which can lead to problems — if not now, in the long run. If we don't have good examples of how to deal with feelings, it's easy to develop harmful habits. Watch out for these negative ways to cope:

- **Denial:** Pretending your emotion doesn't exist so you don't have to deal with it.

- **Withdrawal:** You start pulling away from people and activities you love because you want to avoid something entirely, leading to isolating yourself more often.

- **Bullying:** The saying, "Hurt people hurt people," is very accurate. People who feel good about themselves don't typically engage in bullying behaviors.

- **Self-Harm:** Others turn their anger inwards and desperately seek a release. Self-harm – such as cutting yourself – can sometimes be a way to temporarily numb mental pain by allowing you to focus on the physical pain. If you are self-harming, please speak to a trusted adult immediately.

These harmful ways to manage emotions are everywhere, but they aren't real solutions to anything. Help yourself out of them. Reach out for help.

THE NEGATIVE THOUGHTS: Do You Have ANTs?

Automatic Negative Thoughts, often called "ANTs," are those pesky, spontaneous thoughts that pop up in your mind and make you feel bad about yourself or your situation. An ANT is like a little bug whispering things like, "You can't do it," "You're not good enough," or "What if something bad happens?"

These thoughts happen automatically, often without your realizing it, and can really bring you down. Just like we try to squash annoying bugs, it's helpful to recognize and squash these ANTs to maintain a positive and realistic perspective.

Most ANTs fall under one or more categories:

1. **"Always" Thinking (Overgeneralization):** Making broad conclusions based on a single event or piece of evidence. *Ex*: You mess up one thing and think, "I *always* mess *everything* up!"

2. **Focusing on the Negative (Negative Filtering):** Zooming in on the bad while filtering out the good. *Ex*: Despite all the compliments, you let one criticism ruin your day.

3. **Catastrophizing (Predicting the Worst):** Believing the worst possible outcome will happen. *Ex*: "I missed a phone call; something terrible must've happened."

4. **Mind Reading:** Assuming you know what others think, usually negative, without evidence. *Ex*: "They didn't say hi, so they must be mad at me."

5. **Thinking with Feelings:** Believing something is true just because it feels that way. *Ex*: "I feel useless, so I must be useless."

6. **Guilt Beating (Using "should," "must," or "ought"):** Imposing unrealistic standards on yourself or others. *Ex*: "I should always be on top of things."

7. **Labeling:** Attaching a negative label to yourself or others

based on one incident. *Ex*: "I forgot her name; I'm such a loser."

8. **Personalization:** Believing you cause external events or taking things personally. *Ex*: "My friends are upset; it must be because of something I did."

9. **Blaming:** Assigning blame to others while avoiding personal responsibility or vice versa. *Ex*: "I didn't do well because my teacher hates me."

So, what do you do about your ANTs? Recognizing them is the first step. Once you identify them, you can challenge their accuracy, replace them with more positive or realistic thoughts, or discuss them with someone you trust. This will reduce stress, anxiety, and negativity in your daily life; and if you keep on practicing, it will become second nature to you.

STRESS MANAGEMENT

Life as a teenager can be a whirlwind. A bit of stress is normal and can even be motivating, but too much stress over a long period can seriously affect your health. Effective stress management techniques can help you cope and maintain good mental AND physical health.

Various Stress Factors

- *Academic pressure:* High expectations, exams, and homework can pile on the stress.

- *Social pressure:* Peer pressure, bullying, and the need to fit in can stress you out.

- *Family issues:* Conflict at home or major life changes can weigh you down.

- *Personal challenges:* Relationship issues, body image concerns, and identity exploration can be a rollercoaster.

- *Financial worries:* Money matters can stress anybody out, especially when juggling school work at the same time.

- *Safety and security:* Living in an unsafe environment or a household affected by physical, sexual, or psychological abuse or one that involves *substance abuse* can really amp up stress levels.

How to Handle Stress

- **Take control:** If you can, try to remove or reduce the things causing stress. Some stressors can be managed or eliminated with a little effort. But if the stressor is beyond your control, don't stress out. Just acknowledge that fact, and move on to things you *can* control.

- **Time management:** Learning to use to-do lists and to schedule tasks for school, home, friends, and extracurricular activities can make everything more manageable. (We'll cover time management in much more detail later.)

- **Relaxation techniques:** Deep breathing exercises, meditation, or engaging in hobbies can help reduce stress. Try this: Sit comfortably. Place one hand on your belly and the other on your chest. Take a slow, deep breath in through your nose, feeling your belly rise. Hold it for a moment, then exhale slowly through your mouth, feeling your belly fall. Try to make your exhales longer than your inhales. Repeat this until you feel relaxed.

- **Physical activity:** Regular exercise releases endorphins, improving mood and reducing stress levels. (Another good reason to get your 60 minutes a day!)

- **Healthy lifestyle choices:** Eating a balanced diet, getting adequate sleep, and avoiding harmful substances will help you stay stress-free.

- **Seek help:** Don't hesitate to reach out if stress starts taking over your life. Talk to trusted adults like parents, teachers, or school counselors. Professional help from therapists specializing in teen mental health can be a huge game-changer.

Mindfulness Techniques

Have you ever found yourself all worked up about something that hasn't happened yet? Or maybe replaying an awkward scene that took place in the past in your head over and over? That's because you are not living in the present. That's where *mindfulness* comes in. The idea is to keep you rooted in the present moment.

Mindfulness is all about focusing on the here and now. It's about fully engaging in whatever you're doing without getting caught up in past regrets or future worries. One way to practice mindfulness is through *meditation*. Even a few minutes a day can make a difference. You can also practice mindfulness throughout the day by focusing on your breath, paying attention to your senses, or simply taking a moment to pause and observe your surroundings.

This concept — or variations of it — have been around for centuries in different countries all over the world. It may sound like *hocus pocus* at first, but something about it seems to work for so many people when it comes to calming the nerves and nurturing mental health. Try it!

COMMON MENTAL HEALTH ISSUES

When things get really intense, the issues can manifest themselves in the form of disorders and illness. The three major categories are:

- *Anxiety Disorders:* You know that jolt of adrenaline you feel when you're about to give a speech or ride a roller coaster? That's anxiety, and it's a normal function of your nerves. But for some people, this anxiety doesn't go away and can worsen over time. This can interfere with daily activities and may indicate an *anxiety disorder*.

- *Mood Disorders:* These can include ongoing feelings of sadness, episodes of intense happiness, or swings between extreme happiness and deep sadness. *Depression* and *bipolar disorder* fall into this category.

- **Eating Disorders:** These involve intense emotions, attitudes, and unusual behaviors associated with weight and food. *Anorexia nervosa, bulimia nervosa,* and *binge-eating disorder* are the most common eating disorders.

Remember, mental health issues are not character flaws or signs of weakness. They are medical conditions, just like diabetes or asthma, and they can affect anyone, regardless of age, gender, or background. If you believe you are suffering from any of these illnesses, do not hesitate. Seek professional help.

Dealing with Anxiety and Depression

What are the Symptoms?

Everyone feels sad or down from time to time or worries about a high-stakes event like an exam. But when sadness or anxiety lingers and starts interfering with your everyday life, it's time to pay attention. Here are some red flags to look out for:

- General sadness or hopelessness that lasts for more than a day or two — or is unrelated to anything specific.

- Loss of interest in activities you used to enjoy.

- Changes in appetite or weight. Some people with depression or anxiety feel hungry more often, while others may not want to eat much.

- Changes in sleep. You may suddenly want to sleep all day and dread getting out of bed. On the other hand, you may have trouble falling or staying asleep.

- Tiredness or lack of energy, even after a good night's sleep

- Difficulty concentrating or making decisions.

- Irritability — getting easily annoyed or angry.

- Self-harm or suicidal thoughts.

Coping Strategies

Many coping strategies for minor levels of anxiety and depression are the same as the ones for coping with stress, as they are all related. It is important to tackle depression as quickly as possible so that it doesn't spiral out of control and lead to self-harm or suicidal thoughts.

You don't have to do it alone. Don't be ashamed to ask for help. Mental health professionals can provide appropriate diagnosis, therapy, and, if necessary, medication.

Best places to ask for help:

- Tell a parent, friend, school counselor, teacher, coach, or other trusted adult

- Talk to your family doctor

- The SAMHSA (Substance Abuse and Mental Health Services Administration) Helpline 1-800-662-HELP (4357)

- National Suicide Prevention Lifeline: 1-800-273-TALK (8255)

- The Trevor Lifeline: 1-866-488-7386

- Trevor Lifeline Text/Chat Services, available 24/7 Text "TREVOR" to 678-678

- Crisis Text Line: Text TALK to 741-741

Coping Strategies to Avoid: Drugs and Alcohol

Drugs and alcohol can be tempting escape valves when everything is just too much. Altering your sober state of mind to run away from emotional pain is a short-term fix that doesn't actually fix anything. To work through your emotions, you need to be sober. You can't run from anxiety or depression forever; long-term substance use leads to addiction, worsening every problem you already have.

Studies show that when teenagers have a mental health disorder that goes untreated, approximately 50% of the time, they also end up with a *substance abuse disorder*. The biggest problem with illegal drugs is that **you never know what you're getting or how your body will react**. Many illegal drugs are infused with the deadly *Fentanyl*, for example, to make them cheaper and more addictive, but *you* have no way of knowing that.

Also, some people are more prone to forming addictions than others, so while one person may be able to handle a particular drug recreationally, someone else may develop an addiction to it after just one try. Don't play Russian roulette with hard drugs. It's a losing bet.

To repeat, your mental health is just as important as your physical health. It's a key player in your well-being and deserves your attention and care. You are not alone in this journey; resources and people are ready to support you.

Chapter Four

Relationships & Communication

The World Beyond Your Self

Having learned to take good care of yourself, both in terms of your physical and mental health, you're now ready to engage with the world beyond your own personal space. Relationships are the next big step. These are about connecting with others, sharing experiences, and understanding different perspectives.

But forming relationships is just the beginning – communication is key to making them work. As you interact with more people, from close friends to the wider community, the ability to communicate effectively becomes increasingly important.

Let's explore how to build strong relationships and communicate effectively, expanding your world one conversation at a time.

RELATIONSHIPS: Building Bonds That Last

Life is like a puzzle, and relationships are the pieces that make it complete. They add depth and meaning, but they're not always easy to fit together perfectly.

Types of Relationships

Relationships come in many forms, each with its own set of joys and challenges. There are...

- *Family relationships*, including ties with your parents, siblings, and extended family members. These are often our first relationships, and they play a significant role in shaping our values, beliefs, and behaviors.

- **Friendships** which blossom from mutual affection and the adventures you share together. These bonds are like life's bonus levels—adding fun, offering a shoulder during tough times, and giving you that awesome sense of belonging. Through the highs and lows, friends become your anchor, reminding you that you are valued and never truly alone.

- **Romantic relationships** which involve a deeper emotional connection and, often, a physical one. They can bring a sense of companionship, love, and intimacy.

- Then, there are **acquaintances** and **professional relationships**. These include the relationships we have with our classmates, teachers, mentors, coaches, bosses, or colleagues. They can provide opportunities for learning, growth, and career advancement.

Trust & Respect: Cornerstones of Any Relationships

In any relationship, whether it's with friends, family, or partners, two things stand out as non-negotiables: trust and respect. They're the bedrock of any relationship, whether it's with friends, family, or someone special.

Trust is a bridge between you and another person. It's about feeling confident that they're reliable and honest. When trust is strong, you can be yourself, share your thoughts and feelings openly, and know that they've got your back.

Respect involves recognizing and appreciating the other person for who they are. It means valuing their opinions, attentively listening when they speak, and considering their feelings and decisions. Treat others how you'd like to be treated; that shows true respect.

At the end of the day, for any relationship to thrive, these two elements need to be in place. So, as you navigate your connections, keep trust and respect at the forefront.

Building Strong Relationships

Creating strong and lasting friendships might not be rocket science, but it does demand some attention and effort. Here are some essential tips and tricks to keep in mind — your go-to guide for connecting with others and making friendships that last. These insights will give you a solid start, helping you form bonds that make the high school years and beyond even more memorable.

1. Establishing Mutual Respect: Recognize the value in someone else, honor their choices, and support their individuality. It could be as simple as valuing someone's opinions, even when you don't see eye to eye. It's a mutual exchange: you give respect, and you should expect it in return.

2. Communication: Communication is the heart of any relationship. In the pages ahead, we'll break down the art of communicating, but understand that it's not just about the words you use when dealing with loved ones. Being genuine and clear is crucial. Watch your tone, especially when emotions run high. It's always better to talk and listen with the goal of truly understanding the other person, not just to win an argument.

3. Show Genuine Appreciation: Being appreciated feels good. Period. Appreciation reinforces bonds and deepens connections. Go beyond the generic "thanks" – be specific. If a friend helped you out, tell them exactly how their actions positively impacted you. Authenticity is the key; people can sense the difference between genuine appreciation and insincere flattery.

4. Navigating Conflicts with Grace: Relationships aren't always smooth. Disagreements happen. Yet, it's the approach to resolving these that defines the strength of a relationship. Master the steps covered in the next section: pinpoint the issue, communicate constructively, and seek out solutions that respect both viewpoints.

Building strong relationships requires patience, effort, and an understanding of these essential principles. As you grow and evolve, so will your relationships, reflecting the care and understanding you invest in them.

Conflict Resolution: From Tensions to Connections

Conflict resolution, if done correctly, doesn't weaken ties; it reinforces them. So, how exactly do you achieve that?

1- Identifying the Issue: When disagreements or misunderstandings happen, it's super important to zero in on what's actually causing the friction. Think: Is the tension due to different opinions about something? Maybe a text or DM that got misunderstood? Or is someone feeling left out or unappreciated?

Instead of getting caught up in the drama or making it about "who started it," try to dig deeper to understand the real issue. Focus on the problem, not the person. Once you figure out what's really going on, you're on the right track to sorting things out.

2- Communicating and Listening: In conflicts, clear communication is key. Speak your feelings without casting blame. But equally important is listening. Don't just wait for your turn to talk; genuinely tune in to what the other person is saying. When both sides feel understood, it becomes easier to find a solution that respects everyone's perspective. It's a two-way street: express and listen. (We will dive into more details about the nitty-gritty of communication in the next section.)

3- Seeking "Win-Win" Solutions: Resolving a conflict means seeking a solution that honors the needs and wishes of both parties. Focusing on winning or losing only prolongs the conflict and isn't productive. Compromise is essential.

How do you do this? Start by understanding the other person's needs. What are they really asking for? Then, express your needs clearly and respectfully. The goal is to find a solution that meets both parties' needs. It might require some give-and-take, a dash of creativity, and a sprinkle of patience, but it's worth the effort.

4- Following Up Post-Resolution: After resolving a conflict, take a moment to reflect. What did you learn from this experience? How can you apply these learnings in the future? This reflection is like a debriefing session, where you review the events and learn from them.

Then, check in with the other person. How are they feeling? Is there anything else that needs to be discussed? This follow-up shows that you care about the relationship and are committed to maintaining harmony.

Everyone makes mistakes, but understanding each other's perspective and getting through the rough patches can really take your relationship to the next level.

Drawing the Line: The Power of Boundaries

Boundaries are limits you put in place to protect yourself from being dragged into things you don't want. You're "drawing the line" and letting others know about it, so they don't cross it – intentionally or unintentionally. To stay true to yourself and your values, you must know your personal limits and stick to them. They help you avoid being taken advantage of, manipulated, or pressured into things.

How to set boundaries

1- Trust your instincts: Remember when you felt uncomfortable but didn't speak up? Those were times when somebody was crossing your line. Trust those feelings.

2- Define your comfort zone: Understand what you're okay with and what you're not. Maybe you're okay hanging out with your friends when they are smoking, but you're not interested in smoking yourself. That's your boundary.

3- Maintain digital boundaries: Flirting with someone online might be okay, but exchanging suggestive photos is off-limits. Know where you draw the line, and don't let anyone make you feel bad for enforcing it.

4- Friendships and romantic relationships have limits: It isn't always easy to set boundaries with friends or love interests. But boundaries are needed to ensure you don't get taken advantage of or pushed into things you're uncomfortable with.

Okay, here's the deal: Relationships are a two-way street, and a huge part of that is knowing how to talk and listen. In the next section, we'll break down the ins and outs of communication, giving you the tools to make every connection count.

COMMUNICATION: Making Every Word Count

Principles of Effective Communication

Communication falls into one of three styles: passive, aggressive, or assertive. Understanding these can drastically change how you interact with others.

1) *Passive Communication:* Often used to avoid conflict and keep the peace, this style can make you seem like a pushover or a "people-pleaser" because you rarely disagree with anyone. People might start thinking that your opinions and needs aren't necessary, pushing aside your wants and needs.

2) *Aggressive Communication:* Everyone sometimes loses their cool, but some people use this communication style on a regular basis. It can come across as bullying and tends to turn people off and drive them away.

3) *Assertive Communication:* This is the sweet spot. Assertive communicators express themselves clearly and respectfully. It is characterized by the three Cs: *Clear, Consistent*, and *Courteous*.

Tips for Assertive Communication

- **Use "I" statements** instead of "You" statements. *Ex:* "I feel disrespected when plans get canceled at the last minute" is direct, clear, and assertive.

- **Stick to the facts.** It's easy to exaggerate or resort to insults when upset, but factual communication is far more effective. *Ex:* "You canceled plans three of the last four times, so it's hard to trust you will follow through this time."

- **Practice saying no**. Practice giving a short, simple response. *Ex:* "I'm sorry, no. I would rather not." There's no need to go into long-winded explanations. "No" is a complete sentence.

* **Stay calm.** This can be difficult when discussing emotional topics or when stakes are high. If you can't keep from exploding, yelling, or crying, stepping away and regrouping is probably a good idea.

SITUATION	PASSIVE	AGGRESSIVE	ASSERTIVE
You've planned to see a movie with your friend. When you meet, she suggests joining other friends at the coffee shop instead.	"Sure, no problem. I can watch the movie another time. It will be fun to see everyone."	"Seriously? I've been dying to see this movie. You never care about my feelings! If you want to be with them, fine! Go! Bye."	"I've really been looking forward to seeing this movie, so I'm going to stick to the plan, but you're free to join the others if you want."
Your lab group members have been slacking, and you have been doing the bulk of the work. One of the members asks if you can take on some of their work because they're too busy to do it.	"Yeah, sure, no problem. How much have you completed? None? Oh, that's okay, don't worry. I'll figure it out."	"How dare you? I've been doing most of the work already. I don't care if we fail. I'm done with this group!"	"I feel like I've already taken on more than my share. Everyone should contribute equally. I can't handle any more work."

Passive vs. Aggressive vs. Assertive

Body Language: Speaking without words

Body language refers to non-verbal cues. From the subtle rise of an eyebrow to the hands on the hips, these non-verbal cues can amplify our words, convey deep emotions, or even reveal what's left unsaid.

Facial Expressions:

* **Eyes:** Direct eye contact can mean someone is paying attention, but it can also be a power play to intimidate. Rapid blinking might suggest discomfort or distress.

* **Lips:** Pursed lips can mean disapproval or distaste, while biting lips can mean someone is anxious or uncomfortable. A slightly turned-down mouth can mean sadness or disapproval.

Body movement and posture:

- **Gestures:** Some gestures may seem universal, but sometimes, the same gesture can mean very different things in different places, so always be careful how someone from a different culture might interpret them.

- **Arms and Legs:** Hands on the hips can indicate aggressiveness, defiance, or a show of control. Crossed arms typically indicate that someone is defensive or closed off, and tapping fingers or toes can mean impatience.

- **Posture:** Slumped or slouched can mean sadness, defeat, or lack of confidence, while sitting or standing straight indicates alertness and interest.

By tuning into these cues, you can better understand the emotions and intentions of those around you, leading to richer and more authentic interactions.

Building Listening Skills: The Art of Understanding

Avoiding Interruptions

Let's begin with the golden rule of listening: no interruptions. They break the flow of conversation and can make the speaker feel unheard. So, when someone is talking, let them have the stage. Hold your thoughts, resist the urge to jump in, and let them finish.

Active Listening

This is when you're not just hearing someone's words, but you're really tuned in to what they're saying. It means you're fully focused on the person talking, trying to catch their whole message, including the feelings behind it. It's not just nodding your head; it's showing you get it by giving feedback or asking questions. Doing this can make conversations way more productive and help avoid misunderstandings. Plus, it makes the other person feel valued and heard.

Reflective Listening

This is part of active listening that involves *paraphrasing* what the speaker said, which shows them you're totally tuned into their message. It's not about parroting their words but summarizing their main points and emotions in your own words. It's like saying, "Here's what I heard. Did I get it right?" This lets the speaker know that you're listening to their message.

You can elevate your communication game from a one-way speech to a two-way conversation by honing these skills.

Public Speaking: Owning the Stage

Public speaking isn't just about those moments under the spotlight, microphone in hand, and an audience waiting with bated breath. It might be that toast you give at your cousin's wedding, a crucial presentation in class or at work, or even just sharing an idea in a group setting.

Here's the catch: life's unpredictable, and you never really know when you'll be called upon to speak up. It's a great skill to have and could make the difference between getting and not getting what you want out of life. So let's start preparing!

Overcoming Stage Fright

Let's start with the scariest situation, as everything else would be more casual and easier to handle. Suppose you have to give a speech at a school event or at work in front of a crowd of people. Stage fright can turn even the most composed person into a bundle of nerves. A couple of tips to quiet those nerves:

- **Practice, practice, and practice some more:** Knowing your speech inside and out will boost your confidence and reduce anxiety. The better you know your presentation, the easier it is to stay on track, even when you're nervous.

- **Get familiar with your environment:** Check out the venue before your speech, if possible. Walk around the stage, stand behind the podium if using one, and test the microphone to familiarize yourself with the set-up.

- **Use relaxation techniques:** Before your speech, practice mindfulness, meditation, and breathing techniques to calm your nerves and focus on getting your message across.

It's okay to be nervous. A bit of adrenaline can enhance your performance, making you more alert and energetic. So, embrace those nerves, and take a deep breath. You've got this!

Structuring Speeches

Let's talk about the backbone of your speech: the structure. A well-structured speech has a powerful introduction, a well-organized middle portion, and a strong conclusion.

Start with a powerful introduction to grab your audience's attention. It could be a startling fact, a thought-provoking question, or a compelling story. The goal is to hook your audience and make them want to listen.

Next, present your main points in a logical sequence. Each topic should build on the previous one, leading your audience through your speech like stepping stones across a river.

Wrap up with a strong conclusion that reinforces your main points and leaves your audience with a lasting impression. This is your final chance to impact, so make it count!

Engaging the Audience

What is audience engagement? It's about turning your speech from a monologue into a dialogue. Make your audience feel like they're part of the conversation, not just passive listeners. Here's a couple of tools for this:

- **Storytelling**. Stories create an emotional connection,

making your speech more relatable and memorable. So, weave in relevant anecdotes or personal experiences in your speech to bring your points to life.

* **Audience participation**. This could be as simple as asking questions, conducting a quick poll, or including interactive elements like quizzes or games in your presentation. This keeps your audience engaged by making your speech more dynamic and interactive.

Using Visual Aids

These are like the vibrant illustrations in a book, adding color and context to your words. When used correctly, visual aids can greatly enhance your listeners' understanding, maintain their interest, and reinforce your key points.

You can use a simple slide presentation, a video clip, charts, graphs, or even props. The key is to ensure that your visual aids *support* your message, not *distract* from it. So, keep them clear, simple, and relevant.

Handling Q&A Sessions

A question-and-answer session allows your audience to delve deeper into your presentation to ensure they understand your message. It's also an opportunity to clarify any points and show your expertise.

Encourage questions from your audience, and listen attentively to each one. If you don't know the answer, it's okay to admit it. You can offer to find out and follow up later or direct the question to someone who might know the answer. The key is to handle each question with honesty and respect.

Public speaking is a skill; like any skill, it improves with practice. So, seek out opportunities to speak, whether at a team meeting, a class presentation, or even a toast at a family dinner, so you can get used to being in the spotlight. Each time you step out in front of people, you're honing your skills, building your confidence, and becoming a better speaker.

Navigating Digital Communication

Email Etiquette: Crafting the perfect note

Email is the modern-day letter. It's speedy, handy, and a staple in our day-to-day communication. But just because it's digital doesn't mean manners go out the window. There are rules and protocols for it, too, so here are the basics:

1. Make your subject line clear, concise, and relevant to the content of your email.

2. Address the recipient respectfully. When in doubt, use a more formal title rather than a less formal one, e.g., "Dear Mr. Smith. "

3. Start with a short introduction of yourself if you are writing to someone for the first time, and briefly explain why you are writing them.

4. When writing your message, keep it short and to the point. Break your text into paragraphs for easier reading, and check your spelling and grammar.

5. Don't forget to sign off the email. You can use "Best," "Regards," or "Thanks" for informal emails and "Sincerely" or "Yours Truly" for more formal emails. Follow it up with your name. Add your contact information in your signature so the recipient knows how to reach you.

A word of caution: Watch your tone. Since they can't hear your voice or see your face, the reader can't tell if you are joking or serious, angry or not, unless it is clear in your writing. To avoid un-necessary misunderstandings, re-read your message a few times before sending it to ensure your words really say what you mean.

Social Media Conduct: The Do's and Don'ts

Social media offers a platform to connect, share, and showcase who you are. Yet, as with any public forum, etiquette is essential. So, what are the ground rules?

- **Pause before you post.** Getting caught up in the moment is easy, but once shared, your thoughts become public. And <u>once it's out there, it's out there</u>. So, make sure your post is respectful, appropriate, in line with your values, and truly reflects who you are.

- **Protect your privacy.** Just like you wouldn't shout out your personal details in a crowded street, be careful about what you share on social media. Limit sharing personal details, locations, or daily routines.

- Lastly, **be respectful of others.** Social media is a diverse place, full of different views and opinions. It's okay to disagree, but it's not okay to be disrespectful. Keep your comments polite, considerate, and open-minded.

Online Meeting Protocols

Online, or "virtual," meetings are your portal to the world, connecting you with people across the continent and worldwide without leaving your room. Zoom and Skype meetings existed even before the pandemic, but the pandemic made them the norm. Today, they are a standard way to conduct business meetings, interviews, and classrooms all over the world. Like anything else, though, there are specific protocols and etiquette to follow:

- **Punctuality** is critical. Be sure to log in a few minutes ahead of time in case there are technical issues you need to fix. If you're hosting the meeting, ensure everything is set up right before the meeting time.

- **Keep distractions to a minimum.** Choose a quiet location, mute your microphone when you're not speaking, and avoid looking like you're doing other things on the side.

- When it comes to video, treat it like a face-to-face meeting. **Dress appropriately**, don't fidget, and ensure your background is professional and distraction-free.

- For meetings and classrooms, try not to hide behind photos or initials. **Turn on your video** and show you are there in person, attentive and engaged. People tend to trust people they can see.

- **Stay engaged**. Participate actively in the discussion, show respect when others speak, and focus on the meeting.

So, whether you're crafting an email, posting on social media, or leading an online discussion, make every word, click, and post count. Keep the conversation going, stay connected, and let your voice be heard.

Good communication and relationship skills are your ticket to better friendships and smoother conversations. They'll help you in everything from family discussions to future job interviews. Keep it real, keep practicing, and watch as doors open for you in all areas of life.

Chapter Five

Time Management, Decision-Making & Goal-Setting

Good Habits for Life

E veryone's been dealt the same 24 hours each day. But none of us knows how many days we have in our grand adventure. So, while we're all here, let's make the most of it. Got dreams? Goals? A bucket list as long as a rollercoaster? Perfect. This chapter will help you maximize those 24 hours, make choices with confidence, and set your sights on those big (or small) goals. Let's get to it!

TIME MANAGEMENT

Imagine having an extra hour in your day – time to pursue your passions, excel in school, hang out with friends, or simply relax/sleep without worrying about unfinished tasks. Time management isn't about squeezing more into your day; **it's about finding a balance** that lets you live life to the fullest. Let's look at how you can master your schedule, so you can seize every moment and make the most of your incredible teen years – and beyond.

Understanding the Value of Time

Time is a non-renewable resource. That means once a moment slips by, it's gone forever. So, how can you make the most out of this precious resource?

The Opportunity Cost Concept: In terms of time, *opportunity cost* means that the time you spend on one activity is time that you can't spend on something else. If you spend three hours scrolling through social media, for example, that's three hours you can't use for studying, practicing a hobby, or spending quality time with friends. Being aware of the opportunity cost can help you make better decisions about how you use your time.

The Art of Prioritization: Prioritizing is THE key to time management. You have a limited amount of time each day, so you need to decide which tasks are most important and tackle them first. This helps you to focus on what truly matters, ensuring that your time is spent efficiently, effectively, and productively. The sense of accomplishment you feel at the end of the day will be priceless!

The Time Audit: Want to get a clearer picture of how you are spending your time? Try this simple exercise: For one week, keep a time log. Jot down everything you do during the day and how long it takes. This includes activities like sleeping, eating, studying, hanging out with friends, watching TV, scrolling through social media, etc. At the end of the week, review your log. How much time did you spend on different activities? Were there any surprises? Use this insight to reflect on how well you're using your time and where changes might be needed.

Effective Time Management Techniques

A quick online search for time-management techniques will bring up a long list of techniques, but there are a few that have stood the test of time. Try them out and see which works best for you.

The Pomodoro Technique

Developed by Francesco Cirillo, the Pomodoro Technique is a time management method that encourages people to work *with* their time, not against it. You break your work into 25-minute intervals, separated by a five-minute break. These intervals are known as "pomodori," the Italian plural of tomato.

The process is simple. You choose a task you want to work on, set a timer for 25 minutes, and work on the task until the timer rings. Then, you take a five-minute break. After completing four "pomodori," you take a longer break of 15 to 30 minutes. This method can boost productivity by creating a sense of urgency (the ticking timer) and providing regular breaks to avoid burnout.

You can make it your own by changing the time intervals, but the idea is to not work in intervals that are too long in order to maintain concentration.

The Eisenhower Box

Next up, let's take a cue from the 34th U.S. President, Dwight D. Eisenhower. He was famous for his incredible ability to organize and accomplish tasks. *The Eisenhower Box*, or *the Eisenhower Matrix*, is a simple time management tool named after him.

Picture a simple box, divided into four quadrants. Each quadrant represents a different degree of urgency and importance. Quadrant one is for tasks that are both urgent and important. Quadrant two is for tasks that are important, but not urgent. Quadrant three is for tasks that are urgent but not important, and quadrant four is for tasks that are neither urgent nor important.

	Urgent	Not Urgent
Important	**Do** Do it now	**Decide** Schedule a time to do it
Not Important	**Delegate** Who can do it for you?	**Delete** Eliminate it

The Eisenhower Box

Using this method, you can decide which tasks need your immediate attention (**Do**), which ones you should schedule for later (**Decide**), which ones you can have someone else do (**Delegate**), and which ones you can eliminate altogether (**Delete**). It helps you sort out your to-do list and home in on what's really important.

Time Blocking

Think of your day as a series of blocks. Each block represents a chunk of time dedicated to a specific task or activity. It could be writing a report, answering emails, studying, or even taking a break. The idea is to dedicate uninterrupted time to a single task, rather than constantly switching between tasks.

	M	T	W	Th	F	Sa	Su
6:00-6:30					Sleep In		
6:30-7:00	Walk the Dog	Walk the Dog	Walk the Dog	Walk the Dog		Sleep In	
7:00-7:30	Breakfast	Breakfast	Breakfast	Breakfast	Walk the Dog		Sleep In
7:30-8:00					Breakfast		
8:00-8:30						Walk the Dog	
8:30-9:00						Breakfast	
9:00-9:30							Walk the Dog
9:30-10:00							
10:00-10:30							House Chores
10:30-11:00	SCHOOL						
11:00-11:30		SCHOOL	SCHOOL				
11:30-12:00	SCHOOL					Work	Leisurely Brunch/Lunch
12:00-12:30			SCHOOL	SCHOOL	SCHOOL	6-hour Shift	
12:30-1:00							
1:00-1:30							
1:30-2:00							
2:00-2:30							
2:30-3:00		Homework	Homework				Team Practice
3:00-3:30							
3:30-4:00					Homework		
4:00-4:30							
4:30-5:00	Team Practice		Team Practice	Homework			
5:00-5:30							
5:30-6:00		Work					
6:00-6:30		4-hour Shift				House Chores	
6:30-7:00							
7:00-7:30	Dinner &		Dinner &	Dinner &	Dinner &	Dinner &	Dinner &
7:30-8:00	Downtime		Downtime	Downtime	Downtime	Downtime	Downtime
8:00-8:30		Dinner &					
8:30-9:00		Downtime					
9:00-9:30							
9:30-10:00							
10:00-10:30		Sleep!				Sleep	Sleep
10:30-11:00							

Time Blocking Example

This method not only helps you stay focused but also helps you clearly visualize your daily and weekly schedule.

The ABCDE Method

Now, let's add some alphabets to your time management toolkit. The *ABCDE method* is a powerful technique that helps you organize your tasks based on their significance.

The method is simple. You start by writing down all the tasks you need to complete. Then, you assign each task a letter from A to E based on its importance, with A being the most important and E being the least. Tasks marked with an A are your top priorities, the things you must do. Tasks marked with a B are important but not as much as A tasks. C tasks are nice to do, but not necessary. D tasks are those that can be delegated, and E tasks are those that can be eliminated.

This technique ensures that your attention and energy are focused on the tasks that truly matter.

The Pareto Principle (The 80/20 Rule)

Here's a concept that's a game-changer from an Italian economist, Vilfredo Pareto. He made a keen observation: in his garden, 80% of the vegetables and fruits were produced by 20% of the plants. This sparked the 80/20 rule, or what's known as the Pareto Principle.

In terms of productivity, this translates to the idea that a select few tasks (around 20%) lead to the majority of your results (about 80%). The exact percentages are not important. The idea is to be mindful of which tasks give the most "bang for the buck," so you can prioritize them.

By understanding the Pareto Principle, you can streamline your efforts, minimize stress, and achieve your goals more effectively. Just thinking about it can change your life!

Battling Procrastination

Ever found yourself putting off tasks, only to face an overwhelming mountain of to-dos with little time left? That's procrastination. It is one of the worst productivity killers, and *everyone* struggles with it from time to time. We tend to label people as "procrastinators," as if it's a fixed personality trait, but it really isn't.

Procrastination is more like a defense mechanism, typically against anxieties or triggers that "paralyze" us. There are generally three types of procrastinators among us:

- **The Worrier**: This person is worried about the task, whether they can get it done, and all the things that can go wrong. They feel stressed by having so much to do and lack confidence in their own ability. Their challenge is to be comfortable with risks and focus on the process of learning.

- **The Dreamer**: This person has lots of good intentions but rarely follows through. They love the idea of the finished project, but get annoyed by boring or difficult tasks. Their challenge is to tolerate feelings of discomfort and stop making excuses.

- **The Perfectionist**: This person can be their own worst enemy. They often feel overwhelmed by unachievable goals, believing that everything has to be perfect or it's not worth doing. Their challenge is to find a middle ground and aim for excellence, not perfection.

So what can you do about it? How can you "stop procrastinating," as your parents constantly tell you? Try some of these techniques:

Chunking: "Chunking" refers to the idea of breaking tasks into manageable parts. You break up a big task into chunks of mini-tasks, making the overall task feel less intimidating. Plus, each completed mini-task brings a sense of achievement, keeping you motivated to continue. Rather than organizing your entire closet, for example, start with just the shoes.

Reward System: Rewards are little gifts you give yourself for making progress. Your rewards can be as simple or as fancy as you like. It could be a five-minute break to stretch and relax, a quick game on your phone, a delicious snack, or even a fun outing once a major task is completed. The key is to choose rewards that you truly enjoy. They'll serve as a motivation booster, giving you something to look forward to at the end of the tunnel.

Visualization of Results: Lastly, let's tap into the power of your imagination. Visualization is a sneak peek into a future where your task is already completed. It's about creating a mental picture of the outcome you want to achieve and the steps needed to get there.

Close your eyes and imagine completing your task. How does it feel? What does it look like? How is it benefiting you or others? By visualizing the results, you create a positive association with the task. This can fuel your motivation, giving you that extra push to get started.

Everybody procrastinates from time to time. It's a common part of the human experience. The key is to recognize it, understand it, and take active steps to manage it. You got this.

Juggling School, Hobbies, and Social Life

Managing school, work, hobbies, social life, and relaxation can be like trying to keep five balls in the air at the same time. It's a challenge, right? But with a little planning and boundary-setting, you can find ways to manage them all!

Prioritize and Plan: Use one of the time management tools covered earlier in this chapter to prioritize your tasks. Use planners or digital calendars to block out times for those tasks as well as events to attend. By laying out your week this way, you can visualize it better and manage time more effectively.

Set Boundaries: If you've set aside two hours for study, make sure you're using that time wisely. Turn off social media notifications, let friends know you'll catch up later, and focus on your work. Boundaries aren't barriers; they're guardrails to help you focus.

Quality Over Quantity: When it comes to social life and hobbies, it's not about how much time you spend on them, but *how* you spend it. Two hours spent fully engaged in a hobby or with friends are more rewarding than a whole day of distractions.

Embrace Flexibility: While routines are crucial, it's equally essential to <u>be adaptable</u>. Sometimes, unforeseen events will occur, and that's okay. Learning to pivot and adjust your schedule when needed is a valuable skill.

Time for Yourself: Don't forget to carve out time for relaxation and self-reflection. These moments recharge you, providing the energy you need to juggle everything effectively.

Seek Support: If you're struggling to keep up, don't hesitate to reach out. Whether it's talking to a school counselor, a trusted teacher, or even friends, often others can offer a fresh perspective or practical tips you hadn't considered.

The art of juggling isn't about perfection; it's about balance. Like any new skill, it takes practice and patience. Don't be too hard on yourself if you drop a ball or two at first. Keep going, make adjustments as needed, and soon, you'll be managing your time like a pro in no time.

DECISION-MAKING

Every single day, you're faced with decisions – big and small. Which cereal to munch in the morning, what to wear for the party on Saturday, how to spend your next summer break, which path to take after graduating high school, etc, etc... Decision-making, like any other skill, can be honed and refined by using the right tools and methods and, of course, through practice. Once you master these, you will be able to tackle any decisions with confidence for the rest of your life.

The Process of Effective Decision-Making

Let's walk through a step-by-step process of decision-making that will give you the confidence to make choices you can be proud of.

Step 1: Identify the Decision The first step in effective decision-making is pinpointing the decision you need to make. What are you trying to decide? For example, is it what you want to get out of your summer in general, or do you already know you want to go to a summer camp/program, and you're just trying to decide which one? This should be a quick step, but it helps to keep your focus on what's really important.

Step 2: Explore Options. Once you've defined your decision, brainstorm and list all possible choices without limiting yourself – even wild and crazy ones, because they may help you come up with ideas you never thought of that are actually solid options. Done? Now, cross out any options that are simply too crazy, unrealistic, or just not appealing to you.

Step 3: Gather Information. Time for research! Find out as much as you can about each option that's left on your list. How much does it cost? Where does it take place? When does it start, and how long does it last? Are there hoops to jump through, like applications or interviews? Understand what you need to do to make each option a reality. Depending on how big or complicated your decision is, you may want to use a spreadsheet to organize your information.

Step 4: Analyze the Options. Analyze each option from different angles. What are the pros and cons? Consider the uncertainties in each option, e.g., what are your chances at landing that dream summer job or getting into that fancy program? There might be other factors beyond your control, too, like weather affecting your job earnings at a beach house restaurant. (We'll cover decision analysis tools in more detail next.)

Step 5: Make the Decision. Once you've thoroughly analyzed your options based on all the information available, it's time to decide. Reflect on all you've learned. Which one feels right? Why? In most cases, there is no one "correct" answer. Stakes may seem high sometimes, but you've done your homework, so you are well informed and prepared to make this decision. Go for it.

But, If you don't have to decide right now, and waiting can give you better information or more clarity, that's a valid choice, too. Sometimes, deciding not to decide may be the best decision.

The Classic Decision Analysis Tools

Luckily, we don't have to make decisions blindly. There are several decision-making tools and methods that have been proven to work. They will help you narrow down your options and make it easier to see your choices clearly. Which one to use depends on your preference as well as the type of decision you're trying to make. Give them a try!

Pros and Cons List

Chances are, you are already familiar with this classic, but it deserves the spotlight here because *it just works.* All you have to do is, for each option you're considering, list the good things about that choice (=Pros) and the not-so-good things about that choice (=Cons). It's a simple framework that helps you to consider and weigh all the good and the bad in an organized way.

PROS	CONS
–PERSONAL GROWTH	–LOSS OF ACADEMIC MOMENTUM
–WORK EXPERIENCE	–FALLING BEHIND FRIENDS
–RECOVERY FROM BURNOUT	–MAY LACK PRODUCTIVITY
–CULTURAL EXPOSURE	–FINANCIAL STRAIN

Pros & Cons of Taking a Gap Year

Decision Matrix

The Decision Matrix is just a fancy name for a chart that lets you rate your choices based on different criteria. It lets you compare multiple options against a set of criteria by showing various factors at once in an easy-to-understand way.

Let's say you've received admission acceptances from your top three college choices and now can't decide which offer to accept. Start by listing your decision criteria: tuition, location, student life, etc. Next, rate each college against these criteria. You could use a simple scale of 1 to 5, with 5 being the most favorable. Once you've rated all options, add up the scores. Considering all the factors, the option with the highest total might be your best choice.

	Tuition	Location	Student Life	Prestige	Total Benefit
University of A	5	3	4	2	14
B College	3	5	4	4	16
C University	2	3	3	5	13

The Decision Matrix

While it doesn't decide *for* you, the Decision Matrix can provide valuable insights to help you choose.

Cost-Benefit Analysis

As the name suggests, this one involves comparing the costs and benefits of each option. Let's say you're considering moving out of your family home after high school. The benefits might include more freedom and independence, the chance to check out a new town or city, or a more exciting lifestyle. The costs could involve moving expenses, a higher cost of living, or not seeing your family and friends as much as you'd like.

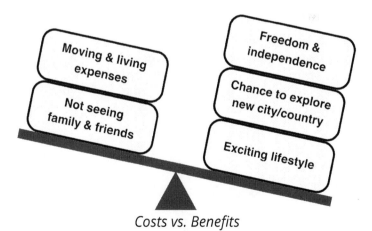

Moving & living expenses

Not seeing family & friends

Freedom & independence

Chance to explore new city/country

Exciting lifestyle

Costs vs. Benefits

The trick is to put a dollar value on these costs and benefits as much as possible or rate them against a scale that is important to you, such as independence. Then, compare the two sides. If the benefits outweigh the costs, the option could be favorable. If not, you might want to reconsider.

These tools won't predict the future or make decisions for you. But they can help you make informed and well-thought-out decisions – which is all anybody can do.

Evaluating the Decision: "Good" vs."Bad"

How did it go? Did you like the outcome of your decision? Wait. Whether the answer is "Yes" or "No," resist the temptation to judge your decision based on the outcome.

It's a difficult thing to do, but you must <u>separate the quality of your decision from the desirability of the outcome</u>. Why? Because you can make a "good" decision, and the outcome may turn out bad, and you can make a "bad" decision, yet get lucky and have a good outcome.

You just can't judge the quality of a decision you made by the outcome. **A decision is good, if you made it after careful consideration of all available information and resources you had at the time you made it.** You must remember that when you made the decision, you were dealing with a lot of uncertainties you couldn't control.

You can't control the outcome. If the outcome sucked, don't beat yourself up. You did your best, and your decision was good. As long as you continue to practice "good" decision-making, you will continue to improve your chances for good outcomes – and that's why it's a good habit to develop.

GOAL-SETTING: Your Personal Compass

If you want to make something of yourself and enjoy life to the fullest, it helps to have goals. Living aimlessly —passively letting things happen to you— is only going to get you so far. But what are goals, and how do you set them?

Long-Term vs. Short-Term Goals

First, let's distinguish between long-term and short-term goals. Long-term goals are your bigger aspirations, like becoming a doctor, starting your own business, or buying a house. Short-term goals, on the other hand, are steps toward your long-term goals. Imagine a timeline. One end is where you are now, and the other end is where you want to be.

As an example, if your long-term goal is to become a doctor, you have to graduate from medical school after graduating from a 4-year college after graduating from high school after finishing all the required courses with good grades. So, your short-term goal would be to finish required courses with good grades. (Everything else might be called "mid-term goals".)

Much like you do with tasks, breaking down a significant goal into smaller goals can help you keep moving forward rather than risk losing momentum.

Setting S.M.A.R.T. Goals

Speaking of which, have you ever set a big, ambitious goal for yourself that you were so excited to work towards, only to abandon it partway through? Maybe you felt the goal was out of reach and got discouraged, or simply lost interest along the way. But with the SMART method, you can ensure your goals aren't just dreams but are achievable targets.

SMART stands for Specific, Measurable, Attainable, Relevant, and Time-Bound. The brilliance of SMART is that it takes a grand ambition and breaks it down into smaller, manageable chunks, and lays out the plan for each chunk using the following framework:

- **Specific:** Clear and concise targets

- **Measurable:** Quantifiable outcomes to track

- **Attainable:** Challenging yet achievable

- **Relevant:** Aligns with your larger ambitions

- **Time-Bound:** Defined timeline

Let's say your big goal is to get on the honor roll at school, except your English grade is pulling your grade point average down. Just saying you want to make the honor roll will not magically pull up your English grade. You need a plan. That's where SMART goals come in.

S	(Specific)	You will raise your English grade from B+ to A
M	(Measurable)	You will track your progress by recording scores of each quiz, writing assignment, and feedback received from your teacher.
A	(Attainable)	You will work with your teacher to identify areas of improvement and set realistic goals for each writing exercise.
R	(Relevant)	A good grade in English will boost your chances of getting on the honor roll and getting into the college of your choice.
T	(Time-Bound)	You have 3 months until the end of the semester to raise your grade.

S.M.A.R.T. Goal for Improving English Grade

Keep in mind, in order to achieve the bigger goal of achieving an A in the class, you may need more than one set of SMART goals besides writing, e.g., reading enhancement or practicing public speaking.

Tracking Progress

As you journey towards your goals, tracking your progress is essential. There are many ways to track your progress. You can keep a goal journal, use an app, or create a visual representation like a progress bar or a goal chart. Make it a habit. Reviewing your progress keeps you motivated and allows you to adjust your plan if needed while keeping you on track.

Celebrating Achievements

Every achieved goal, no matter how small, deserves a round of applause. Celebrating your achievements boosts your morale, builds confidence, and makes the journey more enjoyable. Decide how to celebrate the next milestone, and then allow yourself to indulge guilt-free!

Setting goals helps you see what you want and how to get there, especially as you prepare for life after high school.

Time management, decision-making, and goal-setting aren't just topics to master for now—they're lifelong skills that will continue to serve you well for the rest of your life. With every goal you set and every decision you make, you're laying the foundation for your future. Embrace these tools, refine them as you grow, and you'll be well-equipped to build a successful life.

Chapter Six

Life After High School

Your Journey, Your Options

First thing first. Before you think about anything else, make sure you get your **high school diploma**. Without it, most employment doors will be closed, and you may find yourself with limited options for the rest of your life. If you are unable to graduate from high school the traditional way, take the *GED (General Education Development)* test as soon as you can. Now, after that...?

College? Work? Travel? So many options, how do you choose??

Option 1: COLLEGE

One of the most common routes that teens consider after high school is attending college. It's a tried and true path that many have walked before you. But is it the right choice for *you*?

The Benefits of Higher Education

College offers multiple benefits, each contributing to your overall growth. It's not just about getting a degree, but about expanding your knowledge, honing your skills, and developing as a person. It's about exploring your interests, igniting your passions, and discovering new ones. College is a safe place to experiment, make mistakes, and learn from them.

The *connections* you make in college can also be a huge benefit. Like the pieces of a jigsaw puzzle, your professors, classmates, and alumni network can form a colorful picture of opportunities.

Internships, job placements, mentorship, and friendships are just a few of the possibilities. (Unfortunately, the saying, "It's not *what* you know, it's *who* you know," is truer than we would like to admit in the professional world.)

Also, as the job market gets more and more competitive, a Bachelor's degree is a must-have for many careers and a non-negotiable prerequisite for professional or graduate school programs.

Types of Colleges

There are many different types of colleges, each offering a unique experience: Two-year vs. four-year options, public vs. private, large vs. small, general vs. specialized, etc, etc. Let's take a look.

Community Colleges

These typically two-year colleges offer *associate degrees* and certificates that can lead to employment or be a stepping stone to a four-year college. They're often more affordable and offer more flexible schedules than four-year colleges.

Four-Year Colleges & Universities

These offer a wide range of *bachelor's degree* programs in a variety of fields. They tend to provide a more traditional college experience, with opportunities for on-campus living, extracurricular activities, and a wide range of courses.

Public College/University: These are state universities and colleges that receive public funding and often offer tuition at reduced rates to in-state applicants. Many also cap the number of out-of-state admissions and charge higher fees to out-of-state students. Big cities also have city-funded colleges and universities.

Private College/University: Much more expensive than public colleges, but often offer a wider array of programs and tend to attract renowned professors. These colleges can offer significant networking opportunities that can be valuable when looking for employment post-graduation.

Large Universities: Public or private, these tend to have a wider range of study options than small colleges. They may also be research schools, attracting researchers who are engaged in exciting and innovative work.

Small Colleges: These can be great options for students who prefer a more personalized approach. Not everyone is comfortable in a huge crowd, and the more personal learning experience supported by lower student-to-professor ratios can be a big plus.

Liberal Arts Colleges: These schools focus on providing a well-rounded curriculum in the *liberal arts*, which includes traditional disciplines like English, history, math, and science, but many also offer programs that prepare you for professional fields, including business and pre-med tracks.

Specialized Colleges: Unlike liberal arts colleges, specialized colleges have narrower study focuses. Students typically focus on a discipline that prepares them directly for a specific career upon graduation; for example, schools that focus entirely on music, performing arts, visual arts, business, computer programming, and even sports.

And then, there are military academies, single-sex colleges, and parochial schools associated with particular religions. There are so many options to choose from, so make sure you arm yourself with as much information as possible!

What to Study: Aligning Interests and Career Goals

So what should you study? Choosing a major is a personal decision, and what's right for one person may not be right for another.

Some students know exactly what they want to study. They've always had a passion for biology, a knack for numbers, or a love for literature. Others might not be so sure, and that's okay, too. College is a time to explore. You might start with a general field of study, like science or humanities, and then specialize as you discover what truly excites you. Some colleges expect you to concentrate on your chosen field of study right away, but others give you till your junior year to declare your major.

Consider your long-term career goals. Do you dream of being a nurse? A business owner? A graphic designer? Look at the educational requirements for these careers. What degrees do they require? What courses should you take? Your major should align with your career goals, setting you up on the right path.

Defining Your "Ideal College"

Let's talk about finding your perfect college *fit*. This is not just about academics but about finding a college that aligns with your personal needs, preferences, and goals.

Researching Potential Schools

Start by identifying *what's important to you*. Are you seeking a small college where professors know students by name or a large university bustling with activity? Are you attracted to schools with top-notch facilities, strong athletic programs, or renowned faculty in your field of interest?

Campus culture is important. Are you looking for a college with a strong sense of community, a diverse student body, or perhaps a vibrant athletic or arts scene? What about location? Do you prefer the hustle and bustle of a big city, the tranquility of a rural area, or something in between?

College is not all about learning from textbooks. It's where you grow as an individual, explore your interests, and make lifelong connections. So, take the time to find a college that fits not just your academic goals, but also your personality, lifestyle, and aspirations. You can do this by A) Reading their brochures/websites and online forums —look for details about academic programs, campus culture, student services, housing options, and graduation rates, B) Visiting the campus if possible, C) Consulting your high school guidance counselor, and D) Talking to/interviewing alumni and students of the colleges in question.

Of course, given how fickle the college admissions process is, you shouldn't have your heart set on just one school. Try to figure out what type of school you would like to go to, and come up with a list of several colleges that fit your criteria.

The College Application Process

The college application process in the United States has become maddeningly complicated and competitive in the last few decades. Things have changed _so_ much since your parents went through this process, so you should _not_ totally depend on them for guidance. Plan early, get informed, and seek counsel. Talk to your guidance counselor and search online for advice and extra help. You're gonna need it.

Deciding Which Ones to Apply to

As you consider which colleges to apply to, rank them based on the likelihood of _your_ getting accepted. The common terminology for these rankings includes:

"Far Reach" Schools: These are _extremely_ selective colleges. You can have straight A$^+$s, perfect SAT scores, all sorts of impressive awards, extra-curricular activities, and recommendations, and it would still be a total crap shoot— for _anyone_.

"Reach" Schools: These are also very selective schools, but depending on how well your credentials stack up against the school's "average accepted student profile," you may have a chance. But, admission to these schools, while not impossible, is still a lottery, even if you have the credentials.

"Match" or "Target" Schools: These are colleges where your academic credentials closely align with that of the average admitted student. There is a good chance of being accepted, but it is never guaranteed, so you still have to work hard to make sure your application stands out.

"Safety" or "Likely" Schools: These are colleges with higher acceptance rates, where you are likely to be accepted, either because your credentials beat the average accepted student's or because the school has many seats available; again, nothing is ever guaranteed, but the likelihood of admission is pretty good.

Diversifying your college applications among these categories can help you hedge against the unpredictability of the admissions process and maximize your chances of getting into a college you will be happy to attend. *However,* **don't** apply to colleges you don't want to attend – including your safety/likely schools. You will be just fine, wherever you end up, as long as you have the right attitude and a good idea of what you want out of your college experience.

Prioritizing and Strategizing

The American college admissions process consists of several admission categories, each with its own rules and timelines. Here are the most common ones and their key characteristics:

Early Decision (ED)	• Binding commitment: If admitted, you *must* attend. • The application deadline is typically in early November. • You will receive the admission decision in December. • You can apply to only one school under ED. • But your chances of acceptance become much, much better than in the Regular Decision round.
Early Action (EA)	• Non-binding: You can apply to multiple schools through EA and are not committed to attending if admitted. • The application deadline is typically in early November. • Students receive the admission decision sometime between December and February. • Some schools have a variation called Restrictive Early Action (REA), where you can't apply early (either EA or ED) to any other private school.
Regular Decision (RD)	• Non-binding: You can apply to as many schools as you want and choose among any you are admitted to. • The application deadline can vary, but is typically in January. • You will receive the admission decision in March or April.
Rolling Admission	• Schools review applications as they are received and make decisions throughout the admission season. • Non-binding: You can apply to multiple schools with rolling admissions and choose among any you are admitted to. • Can start in the fall and continue until all spots are filled.

ED or EA has three possible outcomes: *accepted, rejected*, or *deferred*. If you are deferred, your application will be re-considered in the Regular Decision round.

Filling Out the Application Forms

You can apply to individual colleges and universities through their specific websites or use *common application platforms* that are accepted by many institutions. These platforms allow you to input your information, essays, and supplemental materials only once, and submit it to multiple schools. Here are the most notable ones:

Common Application (Common App)	• Most widely used college application platform, accepted by more than 900 institutions in the US and a few outside the country. • You fill out one application and can submit it to multiple schools. • Requires personal information, educational data, standardized test scores (mostly optional), extracurricular activities, and a personal essay. Most schools require additional supplemental essays.
Coalition Application (Coalition App)	• Used by a smaller number of colleges compared to the Common App, but includes many prestigious institutions. • Emphasizes affordability and access, aiming to serve students who may be underrepresented or have limited resources. • Includes a "locker" where you can store important documents and materials during your high school career.
Universal College Application (UCA)	• Accepted by a select group of colleges and universities. • Offers a straightforward application process, and like the others, it allows you to apply to multiple colleges with one application.
Common Black College Application (CBCA)	• Can be used to apply to numerous historically black colleges and universities (HBCUs) at once. • Simplifies the process of applying to multiple HBCUs and encourages more students to consider attending these schools.
System-Specific Application	• Some states and university systems, such as the University of California (UC) system, Texas A&M University system, and the State University of New York (SUNY) system, have their own application portals. (Most of them accept Common App, also.) • Used exclusively for institutions within that particular system.
Individual College Applications	• Some institutions have their own unique application processes and do not use the shared platforms. • These are usually found on the institution's own website.

You'll need to provide details about your background, experiences, and achievements. Be thorough and honest in your responses. This is also where you'll list any extracurricular activities, leadership roles, or community service projects you've participated in.

Gathering Necessary Documents

Most applications will require:

1. Your high school transcript, detailing your academic performance over the years. Make sure you understand how to request school documentation. (In addition to the Common App, some schools use third-party software to request transcripts and letters of recommendation.)

2. Though many schools are dropping this as a requirement, some still ask for your scores from *standardized tests* like the *SAT* or *ACT*. Many institutions allow you to self-report your scores, and then ask for official reports from testing organizations only before enrollment.

Writing a Compelling Personal Statement

Your personal statement, or essay, is your chance to really shine, allowing you to express your unique voice and narrative.

Colleges want to know more than just your grades and test scores. They want to understand your passions, values, and vision for the future. Your personal statement is your opportunity to share these aspects of you.

Be authentic and personal in your essay. Share experiences that have shaped you, challenges you've overcome, or moments that have inspired you. Your goal is to leave a lasting impression, showing admissions officers <u>why you would be a valuable addition to their campus community.</u>

Requesting Letters of Recommendation

Most colleges will ask for letters of recommendation. These are glowing reviews from your teachers, counselors, or mentors who know you well and can vouch for your abilities and character.

Choose your recommenders wisely. Choose teachers you had in junior year if at all possible. (Schools prefer to get the most recent picture of you.) Give them plenty of time to write the letter. Ask them to do this in the spring of junior year or by the start of September in your senior year.

Applying to college is more than just a process. It's an opportunity to reflect on your achievements, clarify your goals, and showcase your potential. So, take a deep breath, trust your abilities, and dive into the application process with confidence. Just make sure you cross all the t's and dot all the i's – and **don't miss the deadlines!**

Paying for College

Evaluating the Costs

Tuition, books, housing, meals, transportation — they all add up. Living expenses can vary greatly depending on whether you live on-campus, off-campus, or at home. Entertainment and miscellaneous spending might seem small now, but they can make a big difference in the total cost. So, how expensive is college?

Are you ready for a sticker shock? For each school you are interested in, go to its website and look up the *Net Price Calculator* to get the estimated cost of attending that particular school, as well as the *Expected Family Contribution*. But don't freak out just yet. You may be able to reduce this cost if you play your cards right.

Many students receive some form of *financial aid*, which can help lower the cost. Investigate all your options - scholarships, grants, work-study programs, and loans. (More on this in a minute.)

Saving Up for College: 529 Plans

A 529 Plan is an investment account with tax benefits that allows you and your parents to save money for your education **ahead of time**, helping to reduce the financial burden when the time comes to pay for tuition. There is more than one type of 529 Plan.

- *Education Savings Plans:* These plans invest your after-tax contributions in mutual funds or similar investments. The account will go up or down in value based on the performance of the investment options.

* **Prepaid Tuition Plans:** These plans let you pre-pay all or part of the costs of an in-state public college education or convert them for use at private and out-of-state colleges.

Ask your parents if they already have one set up for you. If not, talk to them about opening an account as soon as possible.

Reducing Tuition and Fees

Here are a couple of ways to cut down the total cost of tuition:

AP Courses: AP courses are college credit courses you can take while still in high school. They grant you college credits at a significantly reduced cost. When they are applied to a college degree, they can reduce the number of credits you need to take for college graduation, lowering the time and cost commitment on your part. Plus, AP courses look great on a college application and can make your study load lighter in college.

You sign up for AP courses at your high school. Not all courses are offered at every school, and not all colleges accept AP credits, either, so do your research. AP courses do come with an exam fee, but the cost is much lower than taking the same course in college.

CLEP Exams: These are exams you can take to earn college credits at 2900 colleges in the United States. You choose an exam to take from a list of available topics, pay a registration fee plus a test center or proctoring fee, and then take the exam when available. Lists of test centers are available on the CLEP website. Exams are offered year-round. You can earn college credits and reduce your education costs at the same time.

Financial Aid

"Financial aid" is a catch-all term that includes various types of funding you may be able to access to help cover the costs of college education. It includes:

- **Tuition Discounts:** Sometimes offered by colleges or universities to make the cost of attendance more affordable. Some are merit-based, and some are need-based. (Commonly, people say "financial aid" to mean *tuition discounts*.)

- **Grants:** Typically need-based and do not need to be repaid. Common grants include *Federal Pell Grants, Federal Supplemental Educational Opportunity Grants (FSEOG)*, state-specific grants for residents attending in-state institutions, and institutional grants provided by colleges.

- **Scholarships:** Can be merit-based, need-based, or based on other criteria such as specific talents, interests, or affiliations. For example, if you're a whiz in math or a soccer star, there might be scholarships you can get based on that. These do not require repayment, either.

- **Loans:** Borrowed money that must be repaid, usually with interest.

Applying for financial aid starts with the *Free Application for Federal Student Aid (FAFSA)*. Think of it as your financial aid passport. By submitting the FAFSA, you're applying for federal grants, work-study funds, and loans. But that's not all. Many state governments and colleges also use the FAFSA to determine your eligibility for their aid.

Some schools also require you to use the *College Scholarship Service (CSS) Platform* for additional information, in order to determine your eligibility for their own grants, scholarships, and loans.

These forms might seem like a giant hassle with extensive questions about your family's income, assets, and benefits. But don't let that deter you. There are many resources online and at your school to help you navigate this process. **Do a lot of digging.** Talk to your teachers, coach, and guidance counselor.

Negotiating Fees

Yes, sometimes it is possible to negotiate tuition fees and financial aid award decisions with schools. Here's how.

1. **Ask!** Some colleges have a history of being open to negotiation. Send a professional email to either the financial aid office or the admissions office, and make a strong case for why you deserve a discount. **If you've received a better offer from another school, use that as leverage.**

2. **Appeal a Financial Aid Award Decision:** It is possible to make a case for why you should get more financial aid than the school has decided to offer you. Write a professional letter outlining your case.

You might as well give it a try. What have you got to lose?

Evaluating Student Loan Options

If scholarships, grants, and family contributions aren't enough to cover your college costs, student loans can fill the gap. Federal loans, private loans, subsidized, unsubsidized— the options can be confusing.

Federal Student Loans	Generally lower interest rates than private loans. • **Direct Subsidized Loans:** Available to students with financial need. The government pays the interest while the student is in school and during deferment. • **Direct Unsubsidized Loans:** Financial need is not required. Students are responsible for interest payments during all periods. • **Direct PLUS Loans:** These are available to parents of students. The borrower is responsible for interest payments.
Private Student Loans	• Offered by banks, credit unions, and private lenders. • Interest rates vary based on creditworthiness, i.e., credit scores. • Terms and conditions vary by lender.
State-Based Student Loans	• Offered by some states to residents; terms and conditions vary by state.
Parent PLUS Loans	• Federal loans for parents to help pay for their child's education. • Parents are responsible for repaying the loan.

Types of Student Loan

Some of these loans have maximum borrowing limits for each year you are in college, so be sure to note them.

Campus Work-Study Programs: Earning while learning

Lastly, let's consider work-study programs, a unique blend of academics and work. You are given a part-time job on campus where you earn money while gaining valuable work experience. You could be assisting in a laboratory, helping in the library, or even serving food in the dining hall.

These programs not only help you pay for college but also add real-world experience to your resume. So, if you're up for multi-tasking and eager to earn while you learn, work-study programs are a great addition to your college financing plan.

Option 2: VOCATIONAL TRAINING & THE MILITARY

Then, there are vocational or trade schools. They offer specific training in fields like healthcare, technology, or skilled trades like plumbing. Programs are often shorter, more hands-on, and directly focused on preparing you for a specific career. Trades are often overlooked as lucrative career paths, but they <u>can be very high-paying jobs</u> with great health and retirement benefits. Trade unions work to negotiate higher wages and strong benefits for their members. So you may want to make joining one your goal.

Vocational Training

Skilled Trades

Let's start with the skilled trades— think plumbing, electrical, and carpentry. These professions are like the hidden gems of the career world. They might not be in the spotlight, but they're indispensable. After all, who do we call when our faucet leaks, our lights flicker, or our shelves wobble? The construction industry is brimming with even more opportunities, including welding, masonry, and roofing, just to name a few.

Apprenticeships in these trades offer a unique blend of classroom instruction and on-the-job training. You learn from seasoned professionals, work on real projects, and earn a wage while at it.

Healthcare Professions

If you have a passion for helping others and an interest in the medical field, careers like dental hygiene, medical assisting, and paramedics might be your calling.

Vocational training in these fields equips you with the technical skills and practical experience needed to make a difference in people's lives. From assisting dentists with procedures to helping doctors with patient care to responding to emergency medical situations, these professions put you right at the heart of healthcare.

Tech and Digital Careers

If you're tech-savvy, creative, or simply excited about the digital world, careers in coding, web design, or digital marketing could be your playground.

Vocational training in these fields offers a fast-track route into the digital world. You learn the latest tech skills, work on real-world projects, and get a headstart in the rapidly evolving digital landscape.

If you're ready to learn by doing and earn while learning, these paths are worth considering.

Joining the Military

Joining the Military is an option that many students explore in order to both defer college enrollment and reduce tuition fees. All service members are eligible for tuition assistance that is not a loan but part of basic pay. In addition, they can receive up to 36 months of financial assistance for tuition, fees, books, supplies, and housing.

Each of the five branches of the U.S. military – Army, Navy, Air Force, Marine, and Coast Guard – offers training programs, including arts and photography, news and media, aviation, engineering, and health care, among others. Enlistees can receive college credits for their experience and training or can also receive professional and technical training to meet licensing credentials for civilian jobs such as electrical work.

Option 3: THE WORLD OF WORK

Entry-Level Jobs: Gaining experience, building skills

Maybe you want to go straight to work after high school. Entry-level jobs, although often overlooked, are stepping stones towards your career peak. They provide you with the initial experience, skills, and understanding of the work environment.

Even if the first job isn't exactly in your desired field, don't get discouraged just yet. Skills like teamwork, problem-solving, time management, and communication are **transferable and highly valued** across various industries. So, while you're entering data on that spreadsheet or serving those lattes, remember that you're also building a valuable skill set and gaining practical experience.

How to get a job

Once you get some idea of the kind of job you want, it's time to get one. You can look for available positions in the form of online job posts (e.g., Snagajob, Indeed, etc.), local newspapers, or bulletin boards at school or neighborhood coffee shops. You can also approach the employer of your choice directly and ask if they have any entry-level positions open.

The next step is to apply for the job. By the way, the process of applying for a job is pretty much the same, whether it's for a job straight out of high school or summer jobs/internships during college. **So *everybody*, pay attention!**

What's a Resume? What's a CV?

A resume (pronounced *re-zuh-may*), or CV, is a short (traditionally one-page) document that summarizes your background and qualifications. Most employers ask for a copy of it when you submit job applications. So you should have one ready.

Writing a resume as a teenager can be a bit different from writing one as an adult with years of work experience. Search online for examples of what one is supposed to look like. But here are some tips to help you create an effective resume:

Contact Information: Include your full name, phone number, email address, and city or location. You don't need to include your full address.

Objective or Summary: Write a brief statement (2-3 sentences) that summarizes your career goals and what you hope to achieve with the job you're applying for.

Education: List your high school and graduation date. If you have a high GPA, you can include it, but it's optional. Mention any honors or awards you've received.

Relevant Courses: If you've taken any courses that are directly related to the job you're applying for (e.g., computer programming for a tech job), list them.

Extracurricular Activities: Highlight clubs, sports teams, volunteer work, or other activities you're involved in. Mention any leadership roles you've held or significant achievements.

Work Experience: Even if you haven't had a formal job, you can list other types of experience. Babysitting, lawn mowing, dog walking, or helping with family businesses all count. Include the name of the employer, dates of employment, and a brief description of your responsibilities and accomplishments.

Skills: Mention any relevant skills like computer programming, foreign languages, or certifications (e.g., CPR certification).

References: You can include references on your resume, but it's not always necessary for a teen resume. If you decide to include them, list teachers, coaches, or adults you've worked with who can speak to your character and abilities. Or, you can just say, "References available upon request."

Formatting: Keep the format clean and easy to read. Use bullet points for lists and choose a simple, professional font.

Length: A one-page resume is sufficient. Focus on quality over quantity.

Use Action Verbs: Instead of "was responsible for organizing...," say, "Organized..."

Be Honest: Don't exaggerate or lie about your experiences or skills. Be truthful and confident about what you bring to the table.

Proofread: Check your resume for any spelling or grammatical errors. Ask a teacher, parent, or mentor to review it as well.

Remember, your resume is a tool to showcase your potential and what you can bring to a job. Highlight your strengths, and don't be discouraged if you don't have a long work history yet. Your enthusiasm and willingness to learn can be strong assets as a teenager entering the job market.

The Job Interview: Your time to shine

Okay, so you've filled out the job application and submitted it along with your winning resume. Sometime later, they call you to say they want to interview you. Don't be nervous. You got this! Here are some tips for acing your interview:

1. **Research & Prepare:** Research the company and the job position you're applying for. Understand their values, mission, and culture. Review the job description to identify the key skills and qualifications they are looking for.

2. **Practice Common Interview Questions:** Search online for examples of common job interview questions, and practice answering them with a friend or family member. Questions like "Tell me about yourself," "Why do you want this job?" and "What are your strengths and weaknesses?" are often asked.

3. **Dress Appropriately:** Choose professional and appropriate attire for the interview. It's better to be slightly overdressed than underdressed.

4. **Bring Required Documents:** Prepare a folder with extra

copies of your resume, references, and any other documents the employer has requested.

5. **Arrive Early:** Plan to arrive at the interview location about 10-15 minutes early. Punctuality demonstrates your reliability.

6. **Watch Your Body Language:** Maintain good eye contact and offer a firm handshake when you meet the interviewer. These gestures convey confidence and professionalism. Sit up straight, maintain good posture, and avoid fidgeting during the interview. Your body language should convey professionalism.

7. **Listen Actively:** Pay close attention to the interviewer's questions. Listen carefully and take a moment to gather your thoughts before responding.

8. **Ask Questions:** Prepare a few thoughtful questions to ask the interviewer. This demonstrates your interest in the position and company.

9. **Stay Calm and Positive:** Interviews can be nerve-wracking, but try to stay calm and composed. Maintain a positive attitude, even if you face challenging questions. Focus on your strengths and what you can bring to the job. Use specific examples from your experiences to highlight your qualifications when answering questions.

10. **Be Yourself:** Authenticity is very important. Be honest about your skills and experiences, and let your personality shine through.

After the interview, be sure to **send a thank-you email** to the interviewer to express your gratitude for the opportunity and reiterate your interest in the position. And whether you get the job or not, view each interview as a learning opportunity. Reflect on what went well and areas where you can improve.

Remember, practice makes perfect. The more you prepare and practice for interviews, the more confident and successful you'll become. Good luck!

Networking: Expanding your career opportunities

Think of networking as building bridges. Each connection you make is a potential bridge to opportunities, insights, and further connections. Networking isn't just about swapping business cards at formal functions. It's about genuine relationship-building.

Start with your current circle. Your classmates, professors, colleagues, or even family members can all be part of your network. Reach out to people in your desired field. Ask about their experiences and insights. Attend industry events, join online communities, and be active on professional platforms like LinkedIn.

Networking is about mutual benefit. As you reach out to others for advice or opportunities, think about how you can contribute to the relationship, too. You never know how these connections might come into play in your career. As they say, your network is your net worth.

Professional Development

Professional development is how you keep growing and advancing by continuously learning and improving your skills. This could involve attending workshops, taking online courses, reading industry publications, or getting relevant certifications.

In today's fast-paced world, new trends and technologies are constantly emerging. Staying up-to-date and continually upskilling can give you an edge in the competitive job market. Plus, learning new things can keep you engaged and energized in your career.

Professional development isn't a one-time thing. It's **a lifelong process.** So, keep that curiosity alive, stay open to learning, and keep pushing the boundaries of your potential.

Option 4: TAKING A GAP YEAR

A gap year is a break you take after finishing high school, before starting college or a job. (Once you get accepted, you can even request deferred enrollment at a college, securing your spot for later and taking a gap year with peace of mind.) When done right, it can be an awesome experience that helps you grow and discover more about yourself and the world. Here are some things people do during a gap year:

- *Travel Overseas:* Travel offers cultural immersion, language learning, and the development of life skills like problem-solving, adaptability, and independence.

- *Volunteer:* Whether you're teaching English in a rural school, building homes in a disadvantaged community, or conserving wildlife in a national park, volunteering can offer a sense of purpose and a broader perspective on life. Be sure to do thorough research to find reputable, ethical programs.

- *Internships:* Some people get temporary jobs to earn money or work in places related to what they want to study or do as a career. They offer practical experience, industry insights, and professional connections. Not all internships are paid, and some might involve mundane tasks. Finding the right internship requires a lot of effort and a bit of luck.

- *Start Projects:* You can work on personal projects, start a small business, or immerse yourself in hobbies you enjoy.

Make sure you plan and budget your year carefully (some of these options don't come cheap!) — with a clear sense of purpose. If you don't have a good idea about what you want to get out of your gap year, the year will be over before you know it, and you will just end up wasting your precious time. Also, make sure your gap year does not aimlessly stretch out into two, three, or more years. **Whatever you do, do it with a winning plan**.

So, whether you're drawn to the academic life of college, the hands-on training of vocational courses, the practical experience of an apprenticeship, or the adventures of a gap year, know that **there are many paths to success**. Your task is to choose the one that feels right for you and aligns with your interests, values, and aspirations.

Chapter Seven

Money Management

Budgeting, Savings, and Beyond

While you are still living under your parents' roof, you probably don't have to worry about living expenses, and your financial experience is limited to managing your allowance or part-time earnings. But as you seek to become more and more independent in the coming years, you are well-advised to start paying attention to how money works. Getting a handle on the basics now can pave the way for financial wins—even during your teen years—and set the stage for a bright financial future.

THE BASICS

The math is rather simple: Money comes in, and money goes out. If you have anything left over, you can spend, save, or invest it, and if you fall short, well, you have your parents to fall back on for now – but not for too many more years!

Money In: Getting Money

Before you can manage money, you need to *have* money! Do you get a monthly or weekly allowance from your parents? Great. That's something. But if you want more, you need to figure out a way to get more. Making money in high school isn't always easy, especially when you have schoolwork and extracurriculars to worry about. Still, many students use their high school years to work part-time and get a taste of financial independence.

Part-time Jobs: Many businesses are happy to hire students who are willing to work evenings and weekends. Working part-time can provide more than just money. You can gain a sense of responsibility and get experience working with a team. Studies also show that students with part-time jobs that work up to 15 hours per week can even see improved grades. Some part-time employment possibilities for you include:

- Coffee shops

- Fast food restaurants

- Movie theaters

- Grocery stores

- Shopping malls

- Seasonal jobs such as camp counselors, festival workers, water and amusement park attendants, and Christmas sales positions.

(For tips on how to find and get these jobs, check out Chapter 6, Option 3.)

Side Hustles: You can also create your own employment. But do stay away from illegitimate or too-good-to-be-true job opportunities, because <u>illegal or unethical choices can seriously backfire</u>, if not right now, in the future. Consider these instead:

- Dog walking or pet-sitting

- Lawn care

- Babysitting

- Tutoring

- Seasonal chores like decorating houses for the holidays

- Streamer or online content creator

Money Out: Spending Wisely

Every day, you are constantly having to make choices, deciding how to spend your precious cash. The key to spending wisely is simple: Knowing **the difference between needs and wants**.

- *Needs:* These are things you *must have* to survive and function. They include essentials like food, clothing, school supplies, shelter, and healthcare.

- *Wants:* These are things that are *nice to have* but not really necessary. They could include things like eating out, trendy clothes, or the latest and greatest electronic gadgets.

Before making a purchase, ask yourself: Is this a need or a want? If it's a want, consider whether it fits within your budget and aligns with your savings goals. (More on this later.) If yes, enjoy your purchase guilt-free. If not, it might be worth waiting or skipping altogether.

Don't think of spending wisely as denying yourself all pleasures. Instead, think of it as making smart choices that contribute to your financial health and your overall happiness.

Saving: Setting Goals

You know how squirrels stash away nuts for the winter? Saving money is exactly like that. It means setting aside a portion of your income for future use. But instead of nuts, you're saving money, and instead of winter, you're preparing for future goals and unexpected expenses.

Start by setting **savings goals**. Maybe you're saving up for a new phone, a concert ticket, or even college. Having a clear goal can motivate you to save consistently. It's like having a finish line in sight when you're running a race.

Next, consider building an **emergency fund**. This is money set aside for unexpected expenses, like a broken phone or a last-minute birthday gift. An emergency fund is a safety net, helping you handle surprises without stress.

The 50/30/20 Rule

This is one of the easiest guidelines you can follow to start your saving habit. Even if you don't have much money to work with now, it's good to get into the habit of it. And once you get going, keep it up, and it will serve you well for the rest of your life. Imagine your income as a pie:

The Essential Slice (50%): First, take half of your pie. This part is all about your needs, like a roof over your head, food on the table, and clothes to wear. These are the must-haves in life, so this chunk should cover all your basic living expenses.

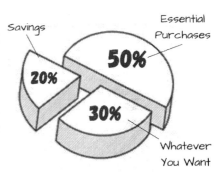

The Fun Slice (30%): Next, grab 30% of your pie. This slice is for all the fun stuff you love, like going to the movies with friends, buying cool gadgets, or grabbing a slice of pizza. It's your spending money for things that make you smile and enjoy life.

The Savings Slice (20%): Now, the last piece of the pie, 20%, is super important. This slice is your savings slice! It's your secret stash for future adventures, big dreams, and unexpected surprises. You can save this money in a piggy bank or, even better, in a savings account at a real bank.

Every little bit counts. Even saving a small amount consistently can add up over time. So, channel your inner squirrel and start building your stash of savings!

Creating a Budget

A budget, for our purposes here, refers to personal financial planning. It's about planning how much money to make, spend, and save. "To budget" is also a verb: You can budget a certain amount of money, say, $20, for a certain item or activity, like a Mother's Day gift. (Hint, hint.)

To create a personal budget, you first need to understand your earnings and spending patterns. Watch your money coming and going over a period of time, say, on a weekly or monthly basis. Get a notebook dedicated to planning and recording your financial activities, and keep a record of every penny coming in and out.

Based on these records, you can start thinking and planning ahead for future spending and saving. Remember those savings goals you set for yourself? Now you can have a better idea of what it would take to achieve those goals and by when.

You can create a simple budget worksheet in a program such as Excel or Google Sheet yourself or, if you prefer, download one of the many free templates available online.

A budget isn't meant to limit your freedom. It's a tool to empower you, giving you control over your money and insight into your spending habits, so you know exactly what you're doing with your money.

BANK ACCOUNTS

One of the most basic tools for managing your money is the bank account. Unfortunately, minors cannot open bank accounts on their own. Some banks have bank accounts specifically for minors, but even those must be opened by an adult, who often will be added to the account as a *co-owner* of the account. Still, it is the best way to learn about money management, so if you don't already have one in your name, you should make it a priority.

There are two major types of bank accounts: *checking* and *savings*. Each serves a purpose, and most grown-ups have both, so let's find out what they are about.

Checking Accounts

They are called Checking Accounts because people write checks based on them for certain amounts of money and give them to other people as a form of payment. The recipient (a.k.a. *payee*) of the check then "*deposits*" the check into their own bank account.

Then, the money gets taken out of the check writer's account and into the payee's account. With me, so far?

Paper checks themselves are going the way of the dinosaurs now that everybody seems to use mobile payment services like Venmo. But checking accounts are still the most common type of bank account that is used to hold people's money that needs to be readily available for *transactions*— i.e., making and receiving payments.

Different banks have different rules for their checking accounts, so if you are interested in opening one, you need to pay attention to the following:

- *Fees:* Bank accounts are not free. Many banks charge monthly maintenance fees for their checking accounts. Others have packages that allow a certain number of transactions per month for a certain fee, and then charge extra if you go over the limit.

- *Minimum Balance:* Some banks require you to keep a minimum amount – ranging from hundreds to even thousands of dollars – in your account in order to waive service fees. There may be other rules, too, like *transaction limits* and check-writing limits, so make sure you can live with them before you sign on.

- *Overdraft Fees*: If your account balance goes negative, meaning you spend more than you have, it's called *"overdraft"* — because you've overdrawn from your account. Your bank will charge you a fee (say, $30) for each transaction that is made while in a negative balance. Or, you will end up *"bouncing"* the check – meaning your bank will refuse to give the payment to your intended payee because you don't have the money to give, and, on top of that, slap you with an *overdraft fee*. Meanwhile, the payee who tried to deposit your check into their account might also be charged a bounced check fee by *their* bank (also typically $30). Now, the payee is mad at you and demands that you pay them the original payment you owe them PLUS the fee they had to pay their bank. That means **you will end up paying $60 extra in addition to the original**

amount! The good news is, many banks offer different kinds of overdraft protection packages, so find out what they are and choose the one that makes the most sense for your situation.

Writing a Check

As I said, check-writing, in general, is on the decline, but there are still occasions when writing a check is necessary, so you should know how to do it. There are various types of checks that individuals can use to make payments or withdraw funds, but for now, you just need to know about a few.

Personal Checks: When you open a checking account, for a nominal cost, you get *checkbooks*. A checkbook is a bundle of checks that you can tear off individually at the perforation and hand over to or stick in an envelope and send to someone as payment. Each time you "write" a check, you fill in the date, payee's name where it says "Pay to the order of," the payment amount in numbers, spell out the amount in words, and sign your name. You can use the memo line to record what the payment was for, but that is optional. Finally, don't forget to record the check's details in the separate register, which comes with the checkbook, to keep track of your spending and prevent overdrafts.

Certified Checks, Cashier's Checks, or Bank Checks: These are checks you have to go to your bank to get issued. The bank first makes sure you have enough money in your account to cover the amount of the check, then issues, for a fee, a special check to a specified payee. Because these are checks guaranteed not to bounce, it is the preferred method of payment for large deposits, like the security deposit on an apartment or a downpayment on a vehicle.

Depositing a Check

If you receive a check as payment, you can *deposit* it into your bank account, either in person at a branch, through an ATM, or using a bank app wherever you happen to be. (If you don't have a bank account, you can find and go to a check cashing store in your neighborhood, but this is not recommended, as these establishments are notorious for charging high fees for their services.)

When depositing in person at the bank, fill out a *deposit slip* (there are some included at the back of your checkbook, and they are also available at the branch) with your account number and the amount of the check. *Endorse*, i.e., sign the back of the check and hand the check and deposit slip to the bank teller behind the window, and they will process the deposit for you.

At an ATM, insert your debit card, follow the on-screen instructions, and insert the signed check into the designated slot. The ATM will scan the check and ask for confirmation before completing the deposit. Mobile banking apps allow you to deposit checks by taking a clear photo of both the front and back of the signed check, which is then submitted electronically for processing.

Don't forget to *endorse* the check by signing the back. Otherwise, it's not official, and you won't get the payment. But also be aware that once you sign a check, it's best to deposit it right away. If you lose an endorsed check and it falls into the wrong hands, someone else may cash it for themselves; it can also leave you vulnerable to identity theft and other financial crimes. In other words, it's probably best not to sign it till you are ready to deposit it.

Savings Accounts

Savings accounts come in more variety than checking accounts. What they all have in common is that the money you have in the account *accrues*— i.e., accumulates— *interest* and grows over time. (I will explain interest rates and how they work a little later.) There are many different types of accounts that are considered "savings accounts," but here, we will cover just a few that are most common and accessible for young people.

- *Regular Savings Account:* This is the most basic type of savings account that banks and credit unions offer. It allows you to deposit and withdraw money as needed while earning a modest interest rate on your balance. It's a flexible option for building an emergency fund or savings for short-term goals.

- *High-Yield Savings Account:* These typically offer a much higher interest rate compared to regular savings accounts. But they usually come with stricter conditions, like high minimum balance, monthly fees, and limits on how often you can make *withdrawals*.

- *Money Market Account:* This is similar to the high-yield savings account but often provides additional features like check-writing capabilities and ATM access. The interest rates tend to be slightly lower than high-yield savings accounts but higher than regular savings accounts.

- *Certificate of Deposit (CD):* CDs are time-based savings accounts where you agree to leave your money deposited and untouched for a fixed period, known as the CD's *term*, which can range from a few months to several years. In return, you typically receive a higher interest rate than a regular savings account. Withdrawing funds from a CD before its maturity date, i.e., when the term is up, can result in penalty charges.

Rules and rates vary from bank to bank, so be sure to compare all the pros and cons before you decide on which account to open.

Opening a Bank Account

Once you have done your research and decided on the account you want, it's time to open one. You can do it in person at a local branch, but most banks nowadays allow you to apply for an account online. As mentioned before, a minor needs to have an adult open an account with them. You'll have to provide some personal information, such as your name, address, social security number, and employment details – and your parent must do the same. Most accounts require an initial deposit, so don't forget to bring your money!

ATMs (Automatic Teller Machines)

Typically, your bank will send you a *debit card* to use to access your accounts on ATMs. These cards often double as debit cards you can use to make purchases just like credit cards. (More on credit cards later.) Basically, you insert this card into the machine, and follow the prompts to check on account balances, deposit checks, transfer money between accounts, or withdraw cash.

When using ATMs to withdraw cash, remember that the fees (usually around $3) are essentially the price you pay to access your own money. To save on these fees, plan your cash withdrawals strategically and reduce the number of times you make withdrawals. For instance, if you anticipate needing $100 in cash to cover your expenses for the week, it's more cost-effective to withdraw the entire $100 at once, for a $3 fee. If you, instead, take out $20 at a time over five transactions, it would cost you $15 in total ($3 x 5) to get the same $100! Also, many banks offer free ATM transactions if you use *their* ATMs rather than other banks', so if possible, look for an ATM of your own bank.

Bank Statements

At the end of each month, your bank will generate a *statement* for your account, which shows all the transactions you made that month, categorizing them as either *credit* (money that came into your account) or *debit* (money taken out of your account). The *balance* is what you have left in your account.

GRINGLOTTS BANK	**Checking Account Statement**

Luna Goodwill
123 Main Street
Anytown, USA 11111
555-555-5555
lsellanuchi@email.com

STATEMENT DATE: 7/31/20XX

Account Number: 123456789

OPENING BALANCE	CLOSING BALANCE
$$$$$.$$	$$$$$.$$

DESCRIPTION	DEBIT	CREDIT	BALANCE
Pay check deposit -- 7/2/20XX		$$$.$$	$$$.$$
ATM withdrawal @ location -- 7/12/20XX	$$.$$		$$$.$$

CREDIT

Many of you are probably still a few years away from having to deal with the subject covered in this section (as you can't even get your own credit card as a minor). But getting a sneak peek at it now will give you a head start on things so you can hit the ground running when the time comes.

Credit vs. Debit

Credit is an addition to your account, while debit is a subtraction. Similarly, credit and debit cards may look alike, but they work very differently. When used responsibly, they both have their place in a sound financial plan.

A **Debit Card** takes money directly from your bank account, allowing you to use only what you already have. It's a real-time transaction tool that prevents accidental *overdrafts*.

A **Credit Card**, on the other hand, works like a short-term loan because you are essentially borrowing money now to pay back later. You can use it to get cash or pay for stuff you want to buy up to your *credit limit*. When you make a purchase, the card's *issuer* – which could be a credit card company, a bank, an airline, or even a retailer like Amazon or Starbucks – pays the merchant on your behalf and records it as money you owe them, i.e., the credit card company. At the end of the *billing cycle*, you pay back the credit card company, basically reimbursing them for all the cash you took and payments it made for you during the past month. If you don't pay the bill in full, *interest* is charged on the remaining balance.

Using credit cards can feel like free money at the moment – until you see how much interest accrues if you can't pay it in full each month. We will cover this topic in more detail in a minute, but first, let's talk about how credit cards work.

Getting Started with a Credit Card

In general, to get a credit card, you need to apply for one, and a decision is made based on factors like income, credit history, and outstanding debts. Once approved, the cardholder -- that would be you -- is given a *credit limit*, which represents the maximum amount you can borrow using that card.

Unfortunately, in the U.S., much like bank accounts, you need to be at least 18 years old to apply for a credit card in your own name – even for *Student Credit Cards*. But there are options you can explore to start dipping your toes into the world of credit cards while still a minor, so if you are interested, you should start looking:

- *Become an Authorized User:* While you need to be 18 to be the primary account holder on a credit card, some credit card issuers allow individuals under 18 to become authorized users on a parent or guardian's credit card account. You will have your own plastic card to carry around in your wallet, but your charges will be put on the adult's bill. Depending on the issuer, you may be able to start building your own credit (more on this later), but you are not legally responsible for the debt.

- *Open a Joint Account with an Adult:* Some banks/issuers allow a minor to open a credit card account with a co-signer, typically a parent or a guardian, who is of legal age and agrees to be responsible for the debt if the minor cannot pay. Both your names will be on the cards, and both your and your parent's credit is affected by how you use the card.

Once you turn 18, you have a couple of additional options:

- **Student Credit Cards:** These were created to help those under the age of 21 build credit. These credit cards are similar to regular credit cards but typically come with lower credit limits and fewer incentives like rewards points. While they are called student credit cards, not all of them require you to be a student to qualify.

- **Secured Credit Cards:** These are a type of credit card that can be easier to obtain for individuals with limited or no credit history, including young adults. These cards require a security deposit, which typically serves as the credit limit, making them feel a lot like debit cards.

Using secured credit cards is still considered borrowing money with a credit limit, so your balance will still be subject to interest charges, but they give you the opportunity to build credit. Debit cards, on the other hand, use your own funds directly from your bank account, do not involve borrowing, and do not impact your credit history. Your choice between the two depends on your financial goals, credit history, and whether you want to build credit or simply manage your own money.

Once you pass the age of 21, credit card restrictions ease, but you still need to show that you have a reliable income source to qualify for any credit card.

Understanding Credit Card Terms

Surprise, surprise! Many credit cards come with various fees, including *annual fees* just to have the cards and sometimes even *transaction fees*. Be careful because cards offering the best rewards or perks tend to also have the highest fees.

Other terms you should know include:

- **Grace Period:** Not always called by its name, *the grace period* is the time between the end of your billing cycle and when your payment is due. For example, let's say your billing period runs from July 16 through August 15. All the charges you made on your card during that period would be listed in your August 15 bill, but the bill says the payment is due September 14. In this case, August 15 - September 14 is the grace period, and no interest is charged during that period.

- *Annual Percentage Rate (APR):* This is the interest rate your issuer charges on any balance you are carrying after the grace period. It's basically the cost of borrowing money on your card. The nice thing is, if you pay your bill in full every month, this cost can end up being zero.

- *Minimum Payment:* This is the smallest amount you can pay to keep your account in good standing. It could be as little as $25 or a percentage of your balance, whichever is higher. But remember, if you only pay the minimum due, you will be charged interest on the remaining balance.

At the end of the *billing cycle* (usually a month), your credit card issuer will generate a statement, much like a bank statement, showing when and where you spent how much. It will also show the minimum payment amount and the due date.

Credit card debts can snowball into massive debt rather quickly, if not managed responsibly. Generations of young people before you have made the painful mistake of letting credit card debts get out of hand and spent years digging themselves out of the financial hole. Don't let this happen to you!

Spending money is fun and easy, but paying it back is a drag and more complicated. Which brings us to...

The Golden Rule: Paying Balance in Full and on Time

Here's the golden rule of using credit cards: **Pay your balance in full** each and every month. Consider this your financial mantra, your guiding principle in the world of credit. By paying your balance in full, you avoid interest charges and stay out of debt. If you don't, that new pair of shoes you bought at a 10% discount may actually end up costing you A LOT more.

If, unavoidably, you can't pay your bill in full, pay as much as you possibly can now, then do your darndest to pay off the rest by the next due date – preferably without putting any more charges on your card until you have paid everything off.

If you forget to pay your credit card bill and don't pay at least the minimum by the due date, you will be hit with a *late payment fee* – typically about $30. Plus, your interest rate might go up, and your *credit score* could take a hit.

To avoid these fees, set a reminder to pay your bill every month. You could mark it on your calendar, set a reminder on your phone, or even set up automatic payments with your bank. Regular payments ensure your financial health stays in good shape.

Building and Monitoring Your Credit Score

Your *credit score* is like a financial report card. It shows prospective lenders (for home mortgages, car loans, other credit companies, etc.) how much they can trust you with credit. A high credit score can unlock benefits like lower interest rates on loans and mortgages, better terms on credit cards, and more.

Credit Score Range

How credit scores are calculated involves so many factors, and it's pretty complicated, so we won't get into it right now. But building a good credit score doesn't happen overnight. It takes time, patience, and responsible credit habits. Establish a solid track record by charging your essential purchases on your card, making payments in full and on time, and keeping your balance low; and don't apply for too much new credit at once.

In the world of credit, certain debt is considered "*good debt*," which helps build your credit score (if managed correctly) like student loans or mortgages because they help you achieve goals whose value will increase over time – like earning a degree or having a place all your own that may appreciate in value. Other debt is considered "*bad debt*," like retail credit card debt or large car loans. This is because this type of debt is associated with either high interest rates or a commodity that decreases in value – like a car whose value plummets as soon as you drive it off the dealer's lot.

Monitor your credit score regularly to keep track of your progress. Many credit card companies offer free credit score access. You can also get a free credit report from each of the three major *credit bureaus*, i.e., Equifax, Experian, and TransUnion, every year.

Understanding credit card terms, paying balances in full, avoiding late payment fees, maximizing reward points, and building a good credit score - these are the basics of using credit smartly and building a solid foundation for your financial future.

INTEREST RATE

Interest rate refers to the percentage rate applied to the starting amount – or *principal* – to calculate the price of having access to that money. In the context of your credit card usage, it would be the additional amount you pay on the balance you owe, and in the case of your savings or investment account, it would be what you would earn on the balance sitting in your account. In that sense, interest is neutral – it can be a friend OR a foe.

If you leave $100 in an investment account that earns 5% a year, you will have $105 by the end of the year; if you have a loan for $100 at 10% APR, by the end of the first year, you will owe $110. That's just simple interest. But the real fun begins with a concept called *compound interest*.

Compound Interest: The Magic Formula

Compound interest works a bit like a snowball rolling down a hill. It starts small, but as it rolls down the hill, it picks up speed and more and more snow, getting bigger and bigger as it rolls. Compound interest is similar. Instead of simply earning interest on the original amount of money, interest earns interest, creating a snowball effect that accelerates the growth of your money over time.

You start with a certain amount of money, known as the principal. This money earns interest. Then, by leaving the principal and the interest you've earned in place, you earn interest on the now bigger amount. In other words, you're earning interest on your interest as well as the principal.

Let's say you have $1,000 in some kind of investment account with a yearly *growth rate* of 5%. After a year, you earn $50, bringing your total to $1,050. In the second year, you earn 5% on $1050, which is $50.25. So, your total after two years is $1,102.50. Notice how you earned more interest in the second year? That's compound interest at work!

Notice in this example that if you just left that $1,000 in your account, it will grow to $1,629 after ten years, $4,322 after 30 years, and a whopping $30,426 after 70 years — without even adding a dime extra.

A word of caution: Remember how I said interest can be a friend or foe? Compound interest can work against you, too. If you carry a balance, i.e., don't pay the full amount due on your credit card month after month, the money you owe can snowball out of control, too.

Year	Total Balance	Interest Earned @5%
0	$1,000.00	$50.00
1	$1,050.00	$52.50
2	$1,102.50	$55.13
3	$1,157.63	$57.88
4	$1,215.51	$60.78
5	$1,276.28	$63.81
10	$1,628.89	$81.44
20	$2,653.30	$132.66
30	$4,321.94	$216.10
40	$7,039.99	$352.00
50	$11,467.40	$573.37
60	$18,679.19	$933.96
70	$30,426.43	$1,521.32

Compound Interest at Work

Other Lessons Learned from Compound Interest

So now that you understand the snowball effects of the compound interest, you can see:

- <u>The importance of starting to save and invest as early as you can.</u> The earlier you start, the more time your money will have to grow. It's like planting a seed and giving it plenty of time to grow into a mighty tree. Even starting with a small amount can lead to significant growth over time, thanks to the power of compound interest. On the other hand, if you start years later, you can invest the same amount of money and not see anywhere near the kind of growth you would enjoy had you started earlier.

- That <u>regularly adding money</u> to (i.e., increasing the principal of) your account <u>will significantly boost your balance</u>. It's like rolling bigger and bigger snowballs down the hill, amplifying the snowball effect of compound interest.

- <u>The wisdom of *reinvesting* your earned interest.</u> This is just a fancy term for leaving all your money, including the interest you earn, in your account and allowing it to earn more interest. It's a simple, hands-off strategy that lets your money work for you. So, sit back, relax, and watch your money grow!

Inflation: The Downer

Before you get all excited about the prospect of $30K as illustrated in the last section, I have bad news for you: *Inflation*.

Inflation refers to the rise in prices of goods and services over time. Let's say the inflation rate is 3% annually. This means that what (let's call it a *'widget'*) you can buy for $100 this year will cost you $103 the next year. Put another way, your $100 will be worth less next year, since it won't be enough to buy that same widget you can buy with it today. (A more fancy way to phrase it would be: The *purchasing power* of your $100 will gradually decline over time due to inflation.)

And that's why stashing cash under your mattress for years is not a good idea. It's better than spending it away on frivolous things, for sure, but you would basically be letting your money wither away in value. Leaving your money in a regular savings account is better, but, unfortunately, not by a lot.

That is because the interest you earn on your money in a regular savings account is generally very low, often under 1%, while the inflation rate can fluctuate from as low as 1.2% to as high as 8%, as it has in recent years. This means the growth rate of your money in the savings account simply can't keep pace with inflation.

You don't need to know fancy math. All you need is to understand that the money in your savings account isn't growing as fast as the prices of things are rising.

This is why it's essential to consider *investment vehicles* that will hopefully let your money grow faster than inflation.

INTRODUCTION TO INVESTING

Getting into investing as a teen may sound a bit premature, but now that you understand the importance of starting early, you can see how knowing about it now can't hurt. Here are some tips:

- **Start Small:** You might not have a ton of cash, but even a little bit can kickstart your journey. Just make sure it's money you won't need right away.

- **Get a Guide:** Having a grown-up mentor, like a parent, to help you set up accounts and make choices is super helpful, especially if you're under 18.

- **Risky Business:** Investing means your money can go up or down. It's a bit like a roller coaster ride, but that risk can lead to bigger rewards. You might lose money, but stay calm. Since you're young, you've got time on your side to bounce back from any dips.

- **Know Your Stuff:** Learn about *stocks, funds, bonds,* and other cool investing stuff. Having a plan and being smart about it will set you up for a bright financial future.

Remember, investing is like planting seeds for a money tree. It takes time to grow, but it can be super rewarding in the long run.

Basic Investment Terms

Stocks, a.k.a. Shares: These are essentially pieces of ownership of companies that are traded by sellers and buyers in the *stock market*. When you buy a *share*, you become a part-owner, or *shareholder*, of that company, hopefully to share in its profits.

You can earn money two ways with stocks.

1. ***Dividends:*** If a company is profitable, it sometimes pays out its shareholders a bonus, called a dividend. You can either take that dividend out in cash form, or use it to reinvest back in the company by buying more shares.

2. ***Capital Gains:*** Stock prices fluctuate over time. If the price of a stock you hold goes up, you can sell it for more than you paid for it, earning you a profit – and that gain is called *capital gains*.

Stocks aren't the only things you can buy in the financial market-place. You can also buy bonds.

Bonds: These are basically IOUs, or pieces of loans, that you can buy to earn interest on them. There are two major types of bonds – *corporate bonds* and *government bonds.*

- **Corporate Bonds:** When you purchase a corporate bond, you are essentially lending money to a company. They agree to repay you what you lent them (the cost of the bond) along with a certain rate of interest.

- **Government Bonds:** These are similar to corporate bonds, but they are issued by a government – federal, state, municipal, etc. – to help pay for public projects like building bridges. *U.S. Treasury Bonds* are considered among the safest and surest investment options, because the risk of the federal government defaulting, i.e., not making good on its promises, is pretty low.

Brokerage Firms: A brokerage firm is a company that connects buyers and sellers to the investment products they are interested in. They make money by charging *commissions* or fees for completing transactions. There are online firms for people who don't necessarily have huge amounts of money to invest that charge lower fees as opposed to some larger brokerage firms that deal mainly with corporate clients and rich people.

Mutual Funds: If you're overwhelmed by the idea of picking individual stocks or bonds, *mutual funds* might be a good idea. Imagine a mutual fund as a basket of various stocks or bonds. When you buy into a mutual fund, you're buying a piece of this basket. It's a way to *diversify* your investments and spread out risk, without having to pick individual stocks or bonds yourself, even though the fees you are charged can cut into your profits.

There are many other investment vehicles and types of accounts, such as life insurance, retirement accounts, etc., that we won't go into here. But I think you've got the picture by now: <u>Investing isn't about getting rich quick. It's about growing your money over the long term</u>. So, take your time, do your research, and make informed decisions. Remember, most investments come with risk, so don't put all your eggs (or your money) in one basket!

TAXES AND PAYCHECKS

Everyone has to pay taxes one way or another, not just adults. Whenever you buy something, like a new shirt, you pay sales tax on that item, for example. But here, we are mainly talking about income taxes. I'm sure you've heard adults around you groaning about them, but think of taxes as a membership fee you pay to be part of your country, state, or city. Taxes the government collects are used to fund public services like transportation, roads, schools, and healthcare. It's a necessary evil and a civic duty.

Income Taxes: W-4, W-2, 1099, and Tax Returns

News flash! The moment you start earning good chunks of money, whether through working or investing, you need to start paying *income taxes* and filing *tax returns*.

Tax returns, despite how the name sounds, are not some kind of reimbursement money the government gives you. It's paperwork *you* have to file every year by April 15 to government agencies. And NO, it's not just for grown-ups. Minors have to pay and file for income taxes, too, once their earnings for the year go over certain thresholds. Let's take this one step at a time.

The W-4

The W-4 form, officially known as the Empoyee's Withholding Certificate, is a form your employer will have *you* fill out when you start a new job. With this, you are telling your employer how much money they should *withhold* from your paycheck for taxes. It's super important because if you don't fill it out correctly, you might end up with too little withheld (and owe money when filing taxes) or too much withheld (and get a smaller paycheck but get *tax refunds* for the overpayment after filing returns). So, you need to strike the right balance. Here's how to fill out a W-4:

Personal information: Start by filling out your name, address, and Social Security Number.

Filing Status: This is about your marital status. It should be self-explanatory.

Multiple Jobs or Spouse Works: This is a bit trickier, so if this applies to you, consult someone who can help you.

Dependents: If you have kids or other dependents, you can claim them here. The more dependents you claim, the less money they'll take out for taxes.

Other Adjustments: Again, if you have any extra deductions or credits you want to consider, you can add them here, but I would advise you to consult someone familiar with your circumstances.

Sign and Date: Just don't forget to sign and date the form.

The W-2

If you're an employee, you'll receive a W-2 form from your employer every year by the end of January for the year that just ended. This form reports your annual earnings and the amount of taxes withheld from your pay according to the way you filled out the W-4.

You will receive a copy of this, and so will the government. You need this to file your income tax returns.

22222	a Employee's social security number 123-45-6789	OMB No. 1545-0008		
b Employer identification number (EIN) 12-3456789			1 Wages, tips, other compensation $$,$$$.$$	2 Federal income tax withheld $,$$$.$$
c Employer's name, address, and ZIP code Employer 1000 Main Boulevard Anytown, USA 11111			3 Social security wages $$,$$$.$$	4 Social security tax withheld $,$$$.$$
			5 Medicare wages and tips $$,$$$.$$	6 Medicare tax withheld $$$.$$
			7 Social security tips	8 Allocated tips
d Control number			9	10 Dependent care benefits
e Employee's first name and initial Last name Suff. Luna N Goodwill 123 Main Street, Apt.7 Anytown, USA 11111			11 Nonqualified plans	12a X $,$$$.$$
			13 Statutory employee [ ] Retirement plan [X] Third-party sick pay [ ]	12b X $,$$$.$$
			14 Other	12c
				12d
f Employee's address and ZIP code				

15 State ST	Employer's state ID number XXXX	16 State wages, tips, etc. $$,$$$.$$	17 State income tax $,$$$.$$	18 Local wages, tips, etc. $$,$$$.$$	19 Local income tax $$$.$$	20 Locality name XX

Form **W-2** Wage and Tax Statement   20XX   Department of the Treasury—Internal Revenue Service

The 1099 ("Ten-Ninety-Nine")

A 1099 form is like a special receipt that shows you earned money from sources other than a regular job. There are several different kinds of 1099s, depending on how the money was earned. If you're an independent contractor or freelancer, you'll likely receive a 1099-NEC form from each client you worked for; and you will receive 1099-INT from your bank for interests you have earned. All 1099s are sent out by the end of January every year, same as W-2s.

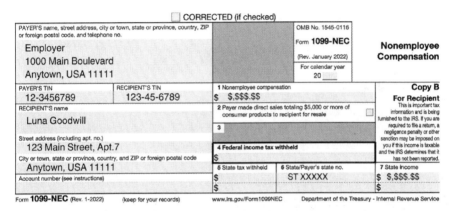

Please know that <u>you can't hide your income from taxation authorities</u>, as they receive copies of the same W-2s and 1099s from your employers, clients, and banks. Sorry!

Tax Returns

Once you have the W–2 and 1099 forms, you can file your tax returns. A tax return is a form you submit to the government that summarizes your income, deductions, and tax payments for the year.

There are multiple levels of taxes you have to pay, depending on where you live. At the federal government level, you at least have to file some type of *Form 1040* to the *Internal Revenue Service (IRS)*. Unless you live in one of the "income tax-free" states, you have to file a state income tax return. Depending on where you live, you may also have to file local, i.e., county or city, income tax returns, as well!

Filling out and filing tax return forms can be a pretty daunting task, even for seasoned adults. Don't be shy about asking for help. Ask your parents or your parents' tax advisor, look for school resources, or look for online tax preparation software that walks you through the process step by step.

Essentially, it's a 5-step process:

1. Add up all your *gross income*

2. Take out various *deductions* you are entitled to in order to calculate your *taxable income*.

3. Then, look up what your *tax rate* is by the *tax bracket* your taxable income puts you in. (10-37%, depending on your income)

4. Calculate your *tax liability*. Different portions of your income are taxed at different rates. There are tax tables and calculators that can help with this calculation.

5. Figure out how much you owe the government by subtracting from your tax liability the amount you've already paid through withholding. (You can find this on your W-2.)

If you end up with a negative number, you've paid more taxes than you owe, so you'll receive a *tax refund*. If you end up with a positive number, it means you didn't pay enough through withholding, so you'll need to pay the amount you owe.

Remember, tax laws can be complex, and various factors can affect your tax liability, such as filing status, exemptions, additional taxes (like self-employment tax), and credits. It's often advisable to consult with a tax professional or use reliable tax software to accurately calculate your taxes.

Your Paycheck and Paystub

Let's go back to your paycheck. How was the amount calculated? The answer is in the *paystub* that comes with the paycheck.

Picture a pizza pie, with different-sized slices representing different parts of your pay. The whole pizza, before any slices are taken out, is your **gross pay**. This is your total earnings before any deductions are made. Now, imagine a few slices of different sizes are taken out of your pizza. These slices represent *payroll deductions* for taxes, *Social Security*, *Medicare*, and maybe contributions to a retirement plan or health insurance. What's left of your pizza after these slices are taken out is your *net pay* or take-home pay. This is the amount you actually receive in your bank account (through *direct deposit*) or via paycheck.

Employer xx-xxxxxxx 1000 Main Boulevard Anytown, USA 11111						**Earnings Statement** Stub Number **123**	
Employee Info			**SSN**	**Pay Schedule**	**Pay Period**	**Pay Date**	
Luna Goodwill 123 Main Street, Apt.7 Anytown, USA 11111			XXX-XX-XXXX	Weekly	Beginning Date to End Date	Jul 31, 20XX	
Earnings	**Rate**	**Hours**	**Total**	**YTD**	**Taxes / Deductions**	**Current**	**YTD**
Regular Earnings	$10.00	40 hrs	$400.00	$$$$$$	Federal Withholding	$$$$$	$$$$$$
					FICA - Social Security	$$$$$	$$$$$$
					FICA - Medicare	$$$$$	$$$$$$
					State Withholding	$$$$$	$$$$$$
					Employer Taxes		
					FUTA	$$$$$	$$$$$$
					SUTA	$$$$$	$$$$$$
YTD Gross $$$$$$$$	YTD Taxes / Deductions $$$$$$$		YTD Net Pay $$$$$$$$		Gross $$$$$$ Taxes / Deductions $$$$$$	**Net Pay** $$$$$$	

YTD stands for "Year-To-Date"

So, next time you get your paycheck, take a moment to look at the pay stub and understand it. Look at your gross pay, your deductions, and verify your net pay. The better you understand it, the more effectively you can manage your money and spot any errors in your paycheck.

As you grow into adulthood, having a good handle on your money can make a lot of things smoother. This chapter gave you the basics, but always keep learning. After all, being smart with your cash means more freedom to do the things you love.

Chapter Eight

Housing & Housekeeping

Independent Living

Graduating from high school is a significant rite of passage into adulthood. Now, as you face the next chapter, a big decision awaits: Where will you live? Whether you're thinking of staying at home a bit longer, moving into a college dorm, or renting your first apartment, let's explore the pros and cons of each choice.

HOUSING OPTIONS POST-HIGH SCHOOL

Living at Home

For many of you, continuing to live at home after high school is a comfortable and economical choice. If you are heading to college close to home or have decided to enter the workforce directly after high school, it can make sense to save money by living at home and commuting daily. For some, it's a tradition to live at home for longer. Living at home also gives you a chance to contribute to household chores, learn to manage your affairs, and perhaps start paying partial rent or help with bills as a way to gradually ease into independence. It's a safe place to start taking on more adult responsibilities while still having a safety net.

Dormitory Living

Living in a dorm, on the other hand, is the quintessential part of the college experience for many students. Imagine a community of your peers, all living together, studying, hanging out, and experiencing the joys and challenges of college life. Living in a dorm offers a unique social environment, complete with organized activities, camaraderie, and a support system of peers. You'll also learn to navigate communal living, respect different schedules, and solve disagreements.

Renting an Apartment Solo or With Roommates

If you crave more independence, renting an apartment might be the right choice for you. You get to create your own living space, set your own rules, and experience what it's like to truly live on your own, or at least away from your parents. Depending on the location, it might save money to rent than pay for room and board at your college. Many first-time renters choose to split the rent with roommates to save money, split the chores, and not feel lonely. However, living with others requires compromise, respect for each other's space, and clear communication about responsibilities and expectations.

Either way, you'll learn to manage rent payments, utility bills, and grocery shopping. You'll also get to tackle cooking, cleaning, and maintaining your living space.

When apartment hunting, remember to prioritize safety and be aware of scammers. Follow these tips to stay safe:

- Look for apartments in <u>reputable, safe locations</u>

- Don't visit apartments alone, and try to avoid going at night

- Don't give more of your personal information than necessary to anyone until you are actually submitting a rental application

- <u>Check with the local police department</u> about the area and things to look out for

When searching for roommates, it's important to find someone who shares a similar outlook on what the day-to-day living will look like. For example, if you are an introvert who is looking forward to a quiet, peaceful living space, you won't want a roommate who plans on partying in the apartment every weekend.

Tips for finding a good roommate

- **Spread the word.** Post a "Roommate Wanted" ad online, using sites such as Roommates.com, or on bulletin boards at local coffee shops. If you are attending college, post on physical and electronic bulletin boards. Many colleges have offices dedicated to assisting students find residential arrangements, so take advantage of them. Also, network with friends, family, and acquaintances to see if they know of anyone who may be interested.

- **Look.** Seek others who are looking for roommates by tapping into the same resources as above.

- **Start early.** It can take time to find the right fit, and you don't want to choose someone who isn't really a good fit just because you are desperate to fill the spot.

- **Be specific.** Share as many details as you safely can about what you are looking for in a roommate, including some of your personal interests.

- **Meet up first.** Meeting a person face to face can give you an impression that online communication cannot. Don't go alone, and <u>meet in a public place</u>. Bring a list of questions about lifestyle, expectations, and general habits.

- **Finances.** Make sure they can cover costs. You can ask about income, or even secure a deposit.

- **Background check.** Ask for and call references to see if there are any red flags before agreeing to share the lease.

Understanding Rental Terms

- **Lease:** An agreement between the renter and landlord. It outlines the specifics of the rental terms and conditions, such as who is on the lease, how long it is for, how much it is rented for, and other details.

- **Lessor:** The person who owns the property and is renting it out – the landlord.

- **Lessee:** The person who is renting the property to live there – that would be you.

- **Tenancy or Term of Lease:** The length of time the rental contract is for. This should also include information about how much notice you need to give to break the agreement, how to renew, etc.

- **Rent Amount:** The amount you will pay monthly, on a specific day of every month.

- **Security Deposit:** This is the amount of money (typically the same as one month's rent) you give the landlord upfront, *in addition to* your first month's rent, that they keep as insurance in case repairs are needed when you move out. If the apartment or house is in good condition, you will get your security deposit back when you move out.

- **Co-Signer:** This is someone who signs the lease with you, like your roommate, and is responsible for a portion of the rent monthly.

- **Guarantor:** This is someone who promises to pay your rent in the event that you can't or won't pay. Often, for first-time renters, parents sign as guarantors.

- **Utilities:** Things like gas, electricity, and water are collectively called "*utilities*." Always check to see if they are included in the cost of rent or if they are separate. They can be a significant extra monthly cost, so be certain before you sign!

In addition, it may not be required by the landlord for you to have it, but you may want to consider *rental insurance*. It protects you in the event of damage from fire, accidents, or even from loss of items due to theft. Rates vary, so shop around for what makes sense for your situation.

CLEANING, ORGANIZING, & DECLUTTERING

The trick to keeping your space clean and tidy is to do a little bit throughout the day, every day, so it doesn't turn into a giant project you have to set aside half a day to tackle. Let's go over the basics of cleaning and organizing that'll keep your home looking sharp and always ready for company.

The Tidy-Up Routine

Consider this daily routine:

1. **Start with making your bed.** It's a small task, but it instantly tidies up your room and kickstarts your day with a sense of accomplishment right off the bat.

2. Next, head to the **bathroom**. Wipe down surfaces, clean the sink, and keep an eye out for any mess that needs immediate attention – like clumps of hair or spilled lotion.

3. In the **kitchen**, make sure dishes are washed and put away, counters are wiped clean, and the floor is crumb-free.

Quick sweeps like these, done regularly, will keep your living space in good shape and prevent messes from turning into formidable piles. Maintaining a clean home is not only about keeping germs to a minimum, but it also helps keep vermins like roaches and rodents away.

The Deep Dive

Every once in a while, your home needs a thorough scrub down. Start from the top and work your way down. Dust ceiling fans, light fixtures, and high shelves using a duster or a dust cloth before moving on to furniture and lower surfaces. That way, you won't have dust falling on areas you've already cleaned.

In the bathroom, give the shower, tub, and toilet a good scrub. Use an all-purpose or bathroom cleaner and a coarse sponge or brush to scrub the shower walls, tub, and sink. Use a cleanser of your choice and a special toilet brush to scrub the inside of the bowl, and use a sponge to wipe the tops and outside of the whole toilet fixture. Clean mirrors and windows using a glass cleaner for a streak-free shine.

In the kitchen, clean the oven, stovetop, and refrigerator. Your kitchen sink could probably use a thorough scrub down, too.

Finally, **vacuum** the carpets and floor. You can even mop tile or hardwood floors if you want to make them really shine.

A solid deep cleaning session might seem like a daunting task, but it can breathe fresh life into your living space and make daily maintenance easier.

Get a bucket or a cleaning caddy that you can pick up at most hardware stores to keep your supplies organized and easy to move from room to room. Must-have cleaning supplies include:

- *All-Purpose Cleaner:* a versatile cleanser that can be used on a variety of surfaces like countertops, sinks, and appliances.

- *Glass Cleaner:* For streak-free windows, mirrors, and lighting fixtures.

- *Bathroom Cleaner:* Specifically designed for cleaning sinks, toilets, showers, and tubs. Look for one with disinfectant properties.

- *Toilet Brush & Cleaner:* Essential for keeping the toilet clean and hygienic.

- *Broom and Dustpan:* For sweeping up dust, dirt, and debris from floors.

- *Mop & Bucket:* To clean and sanitize hard floors like tile, laminate, or hardwood.

- *Vacuum Cleaner:* Ideal for cleaning carpets, rugs, and even hard floors. It should come with an assortment of parts for different surfaces and spaces.

- ***Paper Towels, Microfiber Cloths, and Rags:*** Excellent for dusting, wiping, and absorbing spills.

- ***Sponges & Scrubbing Pads:*** Great for scrubbing dishes and cleaning surfaces that need a bit of extra elbow grease.

- ***Old Tooth Brushes:*** Don't throw away your old toothbrushes. They are excellent for cleaning grouts and other tight corners.

- ***Assorted Trash & Recycling Bags:*** You will be using a lot of these.

- ***Baking Soda & Vinegar:*** These versatile, natural cleaners can also be used for unclogging drains or deodorizing.

- ***Rubber Gloves:*** Protect your hands from harsh chemicals and truly gross things while cleaning

If you have roommates, make sure you discuss shared cleaning responsibilities and routines so everyone pulls their weight. Setting up a <u>schedule for daily, weekly, and monthly cleaning tasks</u> and assignments would be a great way to stay on top of things and ensure everyone is on the same page.

Organize Your Space

Organizing your space is more than just a cleaning task; it's a strategy for smoother, stress-free living. When everything has its place, from your keys to that elusive missing sock, you save time and avoid unnecessary frustration, making your day-to-day life more efficient and enjoyable.

1- Start by **grouping similar items together**: Books with books, clothes with clothes, stationary with stationery. Or, it might make better sense to group things by associated activities: all the school things, all the hobby things, all the camping equipment, etc. Whatever makes sense to you and fits your lifestyle is the way to go.

2- Then, **assign a home for each group of items**. Keep frequently used items within easy reach and store seasonal or rarely used items out of the way. Use organizers, shelves, or storage boxes to maximize space and keep things tidy.

3- Finally, don't forget to **organize paper**. We're talking about the envelopes and documents that accumulate on your desk and every other surface all over your house. Set up a simple filing system that is easy to access so you can file away your bank statements, bills, EOBs, letters from school, etc., as they come in. Even if they are not perfectly in order, having them at least all in one place will save a lot of grief and time down the line.

Oh, and be sure to have all the most important documents –your passport, birth certificate, high school diploma, etc.– together in a secure place. You can get a small safe or fire-proof briefcase for extra safe-keeping of these hard-to-replace documents.

Decluttering

The longer you live, the more stuff you accumulate. It's just a fact of life. But too much stuff can mentally weigh you down, physically take up space, and generally get in the way of life. So, every now and then, it's a good idea to look around and declutter your environment.

- Start by sorting your belongings into four categories: **keep, donate, sell, or trash**.

- Be honest with yourself. If you haven't used an item in a couple of years and it doesn't hold sentimental value, it's probably time to let go.

- Sell items that are in good condition but no longer serve you. Donate items that nobody may buy but could still be useful to somebody.

- Trash items that are broken or worn out.

HOME MAINTENANCE BASICS

Unless you live in a property you own, you can probably call someone – like a landlord, superintendent, or a parent – whose responsibility it is to take care of all home maintenance issues. But it is always a good idea to have the basic knowledge and skills to take care of minor, everyday issues around the home, just in case help is not available right away.

Basic Plumbing Fixes

There are three plumbing issues that even teens can handle: clogged drain, clogged toilet, and running toilet tank water.

Clogged Drain: If the drain in your kitchen or bathroom sink or tub begins to slow or stop draining entirely, you have to remove whatever is clogging the pipe. You can try the following:

- *Boiling Water:* Sometimes, boiling water can dislodge or melt clogs caused by grease or soap scum. Be extra careful while slowly pouring down boiling water.

- *Baking Soda and Vinegar:* Pour ½ cup of baking soda into the drain, followed by ½ cup of vinegar. Let it fizz and work for about 15-20 minutes. Then, flush with boiling water.

- *Plastic Hair Clog Remover:* Made of flexible plastic, this long, slender tool with barbed or toothed edges along its length catches and pulls out hair and debris to unclog bathroom sinks and bathtubs. You simply push it all the way down the pipe and carefully pull it out. Put what comes out in the trash.

- *Plunger:* Place the cup of the plunger over the drain hole, making sure to cover the entire opening. Fill the sink or tub with enough water to cover the plunger's cup. Push down the handle firmly and pull up quickly. Repeat this motion several times.

- ***Drain Snake or Auger:*** You can also remove the drain cover and use one of these plumber's tools, but it is a little more involved. So unless you already know how to use them or someone can show you how in person, I hesitate to suggest you try on your own.

- **Do NOT use** harsh chemical drain clog removers like Drano or Liquid Plumber, as they can damage the pipes.

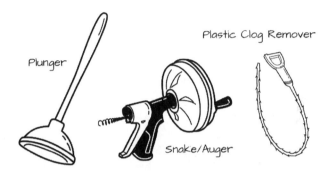

Plunger

Plastic Clog Remover

Snake/Auger

Clogged Toilet: If the toilet stops flushing properly or the level of water in the bowl keeps rising, you've got yourself a clogged toilet.

1. Put on gloves, if you have them, because you may have to come in direct contact with toilet water.

2. Use the plunger:

- Place the plunger over the drain hole at the bottom of the toilet bowl.

- Ensure a good seal by pressing down gently but firmly on the plunger

- Push down and then pull up quickly while maintaining the seal. Repeat this motion several times.

- On the final pull, lift the plunger quickly to break the seal.

After plunging, check to see if the problem is resolved. If it doesn't clear after a few tries, call professional help.

Running Toilet Tank: This is when the toilet tank water doesn't seem to stop after flushing. You can tell something's wrong because you can hear the water running, and you see water continuing to trickle into the toilet bowl. Try the following:

1. Check the flush handle. If it's stuck in the flushing position, bring it back up.

2. If that's not the problem, remove the toilet tank top and look inside.

- Is the chain or rods connecting the metal arm to the rubber flapper at the bottom tangled, keeping the flapper from closing? If so, straighten the chain to let the flapper close.

- Is the rubber flapper stuck open for some other reason? Push it down for now. (Don't worry. The water in the tank is clean.)

Sometimes the handle bar gets stuck. Make sure it's back in the original position. — Handle

Fill valve

Float

Lift rods (or chains) can get tangled or stuck on something. Just untangle.

Lift rods

If the flapper is stuck open, push it down.

Flapper

Overflow tube

Inside the Toilet Tank

If the problem keeps happening, the flapper or the whole valve assembly inside the tank needs to be replaced, so call your landlord or a professional.

In case, for some reason – like water is spraying all over the place – you need to shut down the water in your kitchen or bathroom, it would be a good idea for you to familiarize yourself with the locations of shut-off valves. These are usually located behind or below toilet tanks, bathroom sinks, and kitchen sinks. You just have to turn the handles to shut off the water supply.

Typical Shut-Off Valve

Electrical Safety and Simple Fixes

Working with electricity can be very dangerous, so safety is paramount. All we are going to cover here are fixes that are unlikely to have you come in actual contact with electricity. (Make sure your hands are completely dry whenever handling electrical work.)

There are two minor electrical issues everybody should know how to handle: a blown light bulb and a tripped circuit breaker.

A Blown Light Bulb: Light bulbs have limited lives, and most common household light bulbs, including incandescent, halogen, and fluorescent ones, eventually die. Sometimes, they make a popping noise and blow out while illuminating, and sometimes, they simply refuse to turn on. Either way, don't call your landlord about it. You just have to replace them.

1. Turn off the light switch.

2. Let the dead bulb cool if hot.

3. Get the replacement bulb with the correct wattage and type for your fixture. You can find this information on the old bulb or the fixture itself.

4. Remove the old bulb. Turn it counterclockwise (to the left) to unscrew it from the socket.

5. Screw in the new bulb. Turn it clockwise (to the right) to screw it into the socket snugly, but be careful not to over-

tighten as that would damage the socket or bulb.

6. Check to make sure it turns on, and dispose of the old bulb.

A Tripped Circuit Breaker: If you overload your electrical system, i.e., use too many power-consuming tools or appliances at the same time, you may 'trip' the *circuit breaker*. The electricity on that particular circuit is cut, and all the lights, appliances, and tools plugged into that circuit will shut off.

It's actually a good thing. It's a sign that the circuit breaker is doing its job – which is to interrupt the flow of electricity when the circuit overloads and *trip* (or switch off) to protect the electrical circuit from damage or fire. <u>You just have to find which one tripped and switch it back on.</u>

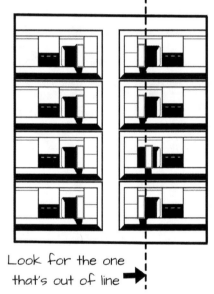

1. Hopefully, you know the location of the electrical panel where the circuit breakers are housed. They usually look like grey metal doors on a wall somewhere near the kitchen – or sometimes in the basement.

2. Open the door, and you will see a bunch of switches which should be properly labeled— "kitchen outlets," "bathroom lights," "hallway," etc. If you are in the right

Look for the one that's out of line ➡

panel, you should see one of the switches in a position different from all the others. (Typically, smack in the middle) That's the one that tripped.

3. Move that switch all the way to the OFF position first, then move it all the way back to the ON position. You are done!

If that doesn't bring your electricity back on, call your landlord or a professional.

Basic Carpentry and Home Maintenance Took Kit

You will need some basic tools for quick fixes and improvements around the house. Tool kits can be purchased at any hardware store, or you can purchase tools individually as you need them. Some must-haves include:

- *Screwdrivers:* A set of both *flathead* and *Phillips-head screwdrivers* in various sizes. (When using, just remember "**righty-tighty, lefty-loosey**"; like jars and bottle caps, you turn right to tighten, and left to loosen.)

- *Adjustable Wrench:* A versatile wrench that can be adjusted to fit different nut and bolt sizes.

- *Hex Keys (Allen Wrenches)*: A set of various sizes. Mostly for bikes and assembling furniture.

- *Pliers:* Combination pliers, slip-joint pliers, and needle-nose pliers.

- *Hammer:* A claw hammer for driving and removing nails.

- *Tape Measure:* For taking measurements

- *Utility Knife:* A retractable, all-purpose utility knife for cutting cardboard, plastic, etc.

- *Level:* A bubble level for ensuring things like picture frames and towel bars are hung straight.

- *Drill and Drill Bits:* Preferably cordless, for drilling holes and driving screws.

- *Saw:* Start with a hand saw and work up to a power saw.

- **Flashlight or Headlamp:** For working in dark or poorly lit areas.

- **Masking Tape & Duct Tape:** For various temporary fixes and packing.

- **Safety Gear:** Safety glasses, work gloves, dust mask, and ear protection.

- **Assorted Hardware:** Nails, screws, wall anchors, and other common fasteners.

Get a toolbox to keep everything together, a ladder or step stool to reach high places, and you're all set!

SAFETY MEASURES AT HOME

Fire Safety and Prevention

Smoke alarms alert you at the first sign of fire. *Carbon monoxide (CO) detectors* alert you to the presence of the dangerous gas. Landlords are required, by law, to have them installed in the kitchen, outside each sleeping area, and on every level of your home, including the basement. Test them once a month to make sure they work, and if not, change the batteries or call the landlord.

Next, arm yourself with *fire extinguishers*. Keep one in the kitchen and any other area where fire risk is high. Learn the PASS technique - **P**ull the pin, **A**im low, **S**queeze the lever, and **S**weep the nozzle from side to side. Look for tutorials on YouTube.

Finally, have an escape plan. Identify two exits from each room, a path from each exit to the outside, and a safe meeting place outside the home. Practice this plan with everyone in the home.

Home Security Measures

Home security is important for keeping you and your belongings safe, but it doesn't have to be scary. Here are some simple measures you can follow:

- **Lock Doors and Windows:** When you're at home or leaving, always lock doors and windows. You can make sliding doors extra secure with a rod or bar so they can't be forced open.

- **Use Peepholes & Chain Lock:** If someone knocks on the door and you're not sure who it is, use the peephole to check and keep the chain lock on if you must open a crack.

- **Keep Valuables Out of Sight:** Don't leave valuable items in plain view from outside the windows.

- **Outdoor Lighting:** Well-lit areas around your home deter potential intruders. Consider motion-activated lights for the front and back yard.

- **Alarm System and Home Security Apps:** If your home has a security alarm, learn how to use it. Some apps can help you monitor your home's security remotely.

- **Create a Safety Routine:** Establish a routine with your family or roommates for checking doors and windows before bedtime.

- **Prep for Emergencies:** Have a list of emergency contacts handy. Mentally plan escape routes in case of fire and other emergencies.

Remember, it's all about being proactive and prepared, not about being scared. Following these measures will keep you safe, so let's not worry about it, and go to the kitchen for something to eat!

Chapter Nine

Kitchen Basics

Eating & Cooking

L iving on your own means cooking for yourself, too! For both nutritional and economic reasons, <u>take-out should be the exception, not the norm</u>. Learning the basics of food preparation, meal planning, and kitchen essentials is the key to healthy living while saving lots of money!

THE ESSENTIALS OF A WELL-STOCKED KITCHEN

Arm yourself with the right cookware and cooking utensils, and you're ready to tackle any recipe that comes your way. Here's what you'll need:

Basic Cookware

- **Non-Stick Frying Pan or Skillet:** Great for everything from sautéing veggies to flipping pancakes.

- **Small & Large Pots:** For boiling pasta, simmering sauces, or making soup.

- **Baking Sheet:** For baking cookies or roasting veggies in the oven.

- **Roasting Pan or Casserole Dish:** For roasting meats or

making large dishes in the oven.

- **Mixing Bowls:** Essential for combining ingredients or tossing a salad.

Basic Cooking Utensils & Supplies

- **Chef's Knife:** A versatile knife for cutting and chopping

- **Paring Knife:** For peeling or cutting small fruits and vegetables

- **Serrated Knife:** For slicing bread, turkey, etc.

- **Cutting Boards:** It's good to have more than one

Chef's Knife   Paring Knife   Serrated Knife

- **Spatula:** For flipping pancakes or burgers

- **Wooden Spoon:** Ideal for stirring sauces or soups

- **Slotted Spoon:** To remove items from liquids

- **Ladle:** For serving soups and stews

- **Tongs:** Great for turning meat or serving salad

- **Whisk:** Essential for beating eggs, mixing batter, or whipping cream

- **Measuring Spoons and Cups:** For accurate measurements of ingredients

- **Grater:** For grating cheese, vegetables, or zesting citrus fruits

- **Peeler:** For peeling fruits and vegetables

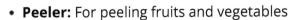

- **Can & Bottle Openers:** For opening canned goods and bottles

- **Colander or Strainer:** For draining pasta or vegetables

- **Pot Holders or Oven Mitts:** To handle hot cookware

- **Thermometer:** Instant thermometers ensure that meat is cooked through to a safe temperature

- **Timer:** To track cooking times. Using a timer can ensure your ingredients cook to the perfect consistency, even if you forget that you are cooking something.

- **Aluminum Foil, Plastic Wraps, and Resealable Plastic Bags:** Mostly for storage; aluminum foil is used in certain cooking techniques as well.

Pantry Staples

Every kitchen needs a well-stocked pantry. To help you keep track of what you have and what you need, consider using an inventory tracking app. Here are some pantry staples to keep on hand:

- **Grains & Starches:** Rice, pasta, quinoa, potatoes, etc.

- **Canned Goods:** Beans, tomatoes, vegetables, and tuna.

- **Baking Essentials:** Flour, sugar, baking powder, and baking soda.

- **Oils and Vinegar:** Oil for cooking, olive oil for low-temperature recipes, and balsamic vinegar for dressing salads.

Spices and Condiments

Spices and condiments are your culinary flavor boosters. They add depth, character, and personality to your dishes. Here's what to stock:

- **Spices:** Salt, pepper, chili powder, paprika, cumin, cinnamon, etc.

- **Herbs:** Basil, oregano, rosemary, thyme, dill, etc.

- **Condiments:** Ketchup, mustard, mayonnaise (in the fridge), hot sauce, and soy sauce

Refrigerator Must-Haves

Last but not least, the fridge. It's where you keep all your perishables crisp and tasty. Here's what to fill it with:

- **Dairy:** Milk, cheese, butter, and yogurt.

- **Produce:** Fruits and veggies for snacking, salads, and fresh herbs.

- **Proteins:** Eggs, meat, fish, cold cuts, and tofu.

- **Leftovers:** Store them properly for quick meals on busy days.

KITCHEN SKILLS

Basic Knife Skills

Whether you're chopping onions for a hearty soup or mincing garlic for a stir-fry, knowing your way around a knife can make your kitchen experience smoother and safer.

Begin with holding the knife correctly. Grip the handle near the blade with your dominant hand and hold the food with your other hand, fingers curled inwards so they are safely out of the way.

Next, practice different cuts - *slicing, dicing,* and *mincing.* Slicing is cutting something into thin pieces, like you'd do with tomatoes for a sandwich. Dicing is cutting food into small cubes, like veggies in a stew. Mincing is chopping food into very fine pieces, perfect for garlic or herbs.

When you are cutting something round that tends to roll around, the first thing you should do is to cut it into a shape that keeps it from rolling to prevent bloody accidents. For example, with an onion, carefully cut it in half or cut one end off to <u>make a flat surface, then put the flat side down</u> on the board to make further cuts.

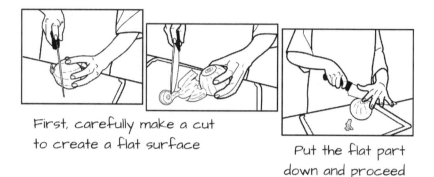

First, carefully make a cut to create a flat surface

Put the flat part down and proceed

Cooking Techniques

Once you've peeled and cut up your ingredients, it's time to turn on the heat!

- First up is **boiling**, the most straightforward cooking method. You're simply boiling a pot of water and submerging food in it, like pasta, eggs, or vegetables. Season the water with salt for pasta. Use the timer.

- **Sauteing** or **frying** is also simple. Heat some oil (or butter) in a pan, add the food, and keep it moving with the utensil of your choice.

- **Deep-frying** is a bit more tricky. You have to heat a lot of oil in a pot up to a certain, high temperature and gently lower food into it. Research thoroughly before attempting, please. Oil burns can be pretty nasty.

- **Baking** and **roasting** can be very rewarding. It's a fantastic, hands-off method for baking cookies and cakes and cooking everything from chicken to veggies. Find a simple recipe, preheat the oven to the designated temperature, pop your food in, set a timer, and let the oven do its magic.

Food Safety and Hygiene

In the kitchen, cleanliness is next to tastiness. Washing your hands before and after handling food is a must. It's the golden rule of kitchen hygiene.

Keep your cooking area clean, also. Wipe down surfaces before and after use. Wash cutting boards, utensils, and pans immediately after use. This helps prevent cross-contamination, where bacteria from one food item spreads to another.

Be mindful of food temperatures. When cooking meat, use a thermometer to make sure it's cooked to the right temperature. Here is a quick look-up chart for internal temperature for meat cooking. (Note that the FDA recommends the minimum temperature of beef to be 145 °F.)

Type of Meat	Medium Rare	Medium	Well Done
Beef	130-135 °F	135-145 °F	160 °F
Pork	145-150 °F	150-155 °F	160 °F
Poultry	Minimum of 165 °F		

Cooking Temperatures for Meat

Refrigerate leftovers promptly. The idea is to maintain the right habitat for your foods to ensure they stay safe and delicious.

Meal Planning and Prepping

Planning your meals ahead takes the stress out of your busy week. Even if you enjoy cooking, having to fix dinner every, single, night can become a real drag really quickly. Do yourself a favor and make it as easy as possible for yourself.

- **Make a rough meal plan for the week**, starting with dinner. Consider your schedule - save easy recipes for busy nights and try new recipes when you have more time. A simple menu plan can include one soup, one pasta, one meat or poultry dish, one fish dish, and one vegetarian dish. Allow for a night of leftovers and maybe pizza on Fridays!

- Stock the pantry and fridge with **easy breakfast staples like yogurt and cereal**. For lunch, make sure you have enough bread, cold cuts, tomatoes, lettuce, and other ingredients for simple sandwiches and salads.

- Finally, **prep ingredients ahead**. Chop veggies, marinate proteins, or pre-portion snacks in your spare time. This will give you a head start to your meals.

Find Simple Recipes to Follow

Websites, food blogs, and social media platforms are brimming with recipes for every taste and skill level.

Look for recipes with clear instructions and short lists of ingredients. As a beginner, start with basic recipes and gradually try more complex ones. Scrambled eggs, mashed potatoes, and spaghetti with tomato sauce are good places to start.

Websites like *Blue Apron* or *Budget Bytes* are geared to absolute beginners in the kitchen. *YouTube* also has a huge selection of cooking channels with step-by-step videos to make following recipes quick and easy.

Recipes are like a guide, not a rulebook. Feel free to substitute ingredients you don't like or don't have. Cooking is all about creativity and making the dish your own. So go on, explore the treasure trove of recipes, and discover your chef within!

GROCERY SHOPPING

Making a Shopping List

Kickstart your grocery shopping with a well-prepared shopping list. Start by taking inventory of your kitchen. Check your pantry, fridge, and freezer to see what you already have.

Now, remember the meal plan we talked about earlier? Time to put them into action! List down the ingredients you'll need for all the meals. This not only prevents you from forgetting important items but also saves you from impulse buys and unnecessary spending.

How to Buy Vegetables

Choosing vegetables that are in season is always advisable for both price and flavor.

- **Leafy greens, cabbage, broccoli, celery, and carrots:** These should look crisp and firm without discoloration. Check and make sure there are no signs of burrowing insects, especially for organic veggies.

- **Potatoes, onions, garlic, ginger:** Should be firm, without a greenish tinge or soft spots, and not sprouting.

- **Eggplants, peppers, cucumbers:** The darker or more intense the color, the riper they are. They should look firm and not shriveled or wrinkled.

How to Buy Fruits

When in doubt, purchase under-ripe ones and let them ripen at home rather than over-ripe fruits that are past prime. But when looking for items that are just right:

1. **Check for firmness.** Don't squish it out of shape, but lightly press on fruits that should be slightly soft when they are ready to be eaten, like peaches and avocados. (Yes, avocado is a fruit —and so is tomato, technically.)

2. **Smell** fruits like melons, peaches, and mangoes. The scent should be floral and appealing. The sweeter the smell, the riper the fruit.

3. **Look at the color.** Fruits like bananas change color as they ripen.

4. **Check for damage.** Bruising, small punctures, insect holes, or white/brown spots are to be avoided. Turn packages of berries to check for signs of mold and rot.

You can find buying guides for specific types of fruits and vegetables online through sites like wikiHow.

Reading and Understanding Food Labels

Have you seen this on food packages?

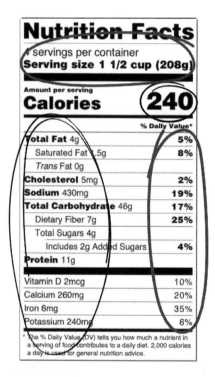

These labels are mandated by the *Food and Drug Administration (FDA)* to give you information about ingredients, serving sizes, and nutritional values contained in food items.

Start with the **serving size** info at the top. A serving size is the benchmark all the other numbers are based on. It tells you how big a single serving is and how many servings are contained in the package.

Next, check out the **calories**. It tells you how much energy you get from one serving. If you're watching your weight, this number is especially important.

The **nutrients** are listed next, like the ingredients in a recipe. Some, like *fiber* and *vitamins*, you want to consume as much as you can. Others, like *sodium* and *saturated fat*, should be consumed in smaller amounts.

Lastly, the percent **Daily Value (%DV)** listing tells you how much of each important nutrient one serving of that food contributes to a total daily diet. The percentages are based on a recommended 2,000-calorie daily diet for an adult. For example, if it says a package of tofu contains 1g of Dietary Fiber or 4%, it means one serving of that tofu gives you 4% of dietary fiber that is recommended for an adult to get *per day*.

Dates on Food Packages

Watch out. There are different kinds of dates on food packages, and it can get a little confusing:

- *Sell By:* This is for the store, telling them by which date an item should be sold or removed from the shelf, mainly for inventory management. If products have been stored properly, they should be safe to consume even after this date.

- *Best If Used By/Best Before:* This indicates until which date the product is expected to be at its best quality. It is not a safety date, and many foods, particularly non-perishable goods, can still be safely consumed past this date, though they may not taste or perform their best.

- *Use By:* This is typically found on perishable foods, and tells you the last date recommended for the use of the product at peak quality. After this date, safety can quickly become questionable.

- *Expiration Date:* The date after which the product is not guaranteed to maintain its intended qualities and characteristics. Consumption after this date is not advisable.

Eating spoiled food can be more than just unpleasant; it can be dangerous. Always check these dates on packages, but trust your senses. If the texture is off, the food is slimy or has discoloration, smells or tastes bad, then trash it, no matter what the date label says. Shellfish and poultry can be particularly dangerous if prepared improperly or consumed past their prime.

Sales and Discounts

Stores often have weekly sales, so keep an eye out for flyers and signs. But don't be tricked into buying something you don't need.

Remember, <u>it's not a bargain if you can't use it before it spoils</u>. Also, be wary of deals like "buy one, get one 50% off." Make sure to do the math to see if it's really a good deal.

Storing Food

So you've come home with bags of groceries. Do you know how to store them properly? Let's go through the basics:

- **Dry and Non-Perishable Goods** (like pasta, rice, canned foods, and snacks): Keep in a cool, dry place away from direct sunlight. Use airtight containers to prevent pests.

- **Perishables** (dairy products, meats, poultry, and seafood): Store in the refrigerator at or below 40°F. Raw meat and seafood should be sealed in containers.

- **Vegetables and Fruits:** Go by how they were sold in stores. Items that were refrigerated or kept on cooled racks, like leafy vegetables, should go in the crisper drawer of the fridge; items that were out in the open, like potatoes and onions, should be kept in a cool, dark place, like the pantry. But even items that were not refrigerated in the store, like berries and tomatoes, should be moved to the fridge if they have peaked in quality but are not going to be consumed right away.

- **Freeze** items you won't use anytime soon, like extra bread, meat, and leftovers. Use airtight containers or freezer bags to prevent freezer burn. It's a good idea to label items with the date so you know what they are and how long they have been in the freezer.

- **Leftovers:** Store leftovers in tightly covered containers and refrigerate them within two hours of cooking.

Here are a few more things to keep in mind:

- Invest in **reusable storage bags and containers**. They are environmentally friendly AND save you money.

- **Avoid overpacking.** Don't overpack your fridge or freezer.

Proper air circulation is necessary to maintain safe and consistent temperatures.

- **Rotate items.** When stocking your pantry or refrigerator, place newer items behind old ones. This makes sure you use older items first, reducing food waste.

THE APPLIANCE NO-NOS

Lastly, I can't leave the kitchen chapter without warning you against these appliance taboos. Dishwashers and microwave ovens are super convenient devices, but there are definitely things that don't belong inside them. Here are the most important items for you to know—to protect your wares and ensure safety.

Things that shouldn't go into the dishwasher

You should avoid putting certain things in the dishwasher due to the risk of damage, wear, or other issues. Here's the basic list:

- **Wooden Items:** Wood can warp, crack, or lose its finish.

- **Cast Iron Pans:** The seasoning can be stripped off the pan.

- **Nonstick Pans:** The nonstick coating can wear off over time.

- **Aluminum Items:** They can discolor and become dull or misshapen.

- **Gold, Brass, Bronze, Pewter, and Copper Items:** These can tarnish.

- **Sharp Knives:** The blades can get dull.

- **Certain Plastics:** Some plastics can warp or melt.

- **Anything Delicate or Valuable**, including crystal, hand-painted ceramics, and pottery: They can chip, crack, or change colors. Don't risk it, or you may be sorry.

It's always a good idea to check the manufacturer's care instructions. When in doubt, it's best to hand wash.

Things that shouldn't go into the microwave oven

Microwaving certain items can be unsafe to you or damaging to the microwave or the items themselves. These include:

- **Metal,** including aluminum foil and wares with metallic trim: These can cause a fire or damage the microwave. Sparks can fly!

- **Plastic Containers** not labeled "Microwave Safe": Some plastic can melt or release harmful chemicals when heated.

- **Styrofoam Containers:** They can melt and release harmful chemicals.

- **Eggs in Shells, Fruits/Vegetables with Skin, and Food in Sealed Containers:** They can explode without holes or an opening to release built-up steam.

- **Dry Sponges, Dishcloths, or Nothing:** Without moisture to absorb the microwave energy, dry items can catch fire; running it empty can cause damage to the microwave itself.

Always ensure you're using microwave-safe containers. If unsure, consult the manufacturer's guidelines or heat your food another way.

With kitchen basics under your belt, you're set to tackle the stove and the store like a pro. Armed with the essential information on cookware, shopping smarts, and cooking techniques, you're ready to whip up meals that are as tasty as they are nourishing. *Bon appétit!*

Chapter Ten

Clothing Care

Keeping Your Threads Fresh

C lothes say a lot about you, and looking good doesn't come cheap. Treat your clothes right, and they'll last much longer, which means more money for the stuff you really want. Time to get the hang of doing your own laundry—your style (and your wallet) will thank you for it. It's a simple skill that'll pay off big time, especially when you're out on your own.

LAUNDRY

Decoding Laundry Symbols

Most clothing items come with tags that tell you what type of fabric they are made of and how they should be cared for. Many caring instructions are written in plain English, but a lot of others have cryptic symbols on them. What do they mean? Well, you're gonna find out... Right now!

Washing Symbols

Washing symbols, those little tub-like icons, literally *show* you how to wash your clothes. It's important to follow these instructions because if you don't, you can ruin your clothes pretty badly. Washing the wrong thing in water that's too hot, for example, can end up shrinking it or, worse, its color can bleed, <u>ruining everything else you washed with it</u>. Delicate fabrics can pull or rip if washed on a cycle that isn't gentle enough.

A tub symbol with a number inside indicates the maximum temperature at which an item can be washed. A hand-in-the-tub symbol means that the item should be hand-washed. A crossed-out tub means washing is not allowed! Sometimes an item can be dry-cleaned only, and will typically have that mentioned on the label. If that's the case, take the item to your neighborhood dry cleaner.

Drying Symbols

Drying symbols are squares with various icons inside. Same as washing, you'd better pay attention to the drying instructions. Heat too high can shrink clothing, cause pilling or felting of knit fabrics, and cause other fabrics to lose shape or even crack – like the lettering or designs on graphic t-shirts.

A square with a circle inside means you can use the dryer. Black circle means tumble dry with no heat. Dots inside the circle represent the heat levels - one for low, two for medium, and three for high. Squares with various lines without circles indicate recommendations for natural air drying, including hang dry, flat dry, dry in the shade, etc.

Ironing Symbols

These look like a little old-fashioned iron. An iron symbol with dots indicates the temperature setting on your iron. No dots means any temperature is fine, one dot for low, two for medium, and three for high. A crossed-out iron means that you cannot safely iron the item. Note that <u>cotton and linen are the only types of fabric that dampening or steaming is recommended for</u>. You should not use the steam function on your iron for other fabrics.

Bleaching Symbols

A plain triangle means your clothes can be bleached safely. A triangle with stripes means only non-chlorine bleach is okay. A crossed-out triangle means that bleach of any kind will ruin the item.

Dry Cleaning Symbols

A plain circle means dry-cleaning is okay. A letter inside the circle lets the dry cleaner know what solvent to use. A crossed-out circle means that an item should *not* be dry-cleaned. Sometimes, an article will have a label that simply says, 'Dry Clean Only.'

Washing, Drying, and Ironing

Now that you know what to do with your clothes, let's do it.

Sorting Laundry: The First Step

Look inside your laundry basket. Is it a mishmash of all the clothes you've worn throughout the week? They are different colors, fabrics, and weights, right? Knowing what you know now about different laundry requirements for different types of clothes, would you want to toss them all together in one load? Can you see the potential for disaster? <u>That's why you have to sort them.</u>

Separate your whites, light colors, and darks into three piles. These are your three loads of laundry. This not only prevents colors from bleeding onto each other but also allows you to adjust the wash settings for each pile. Whites love hot water, while colors prefer it cold. Delicate fabrics like silk or lace may need a gentler cycle or even a hand wash. Check labels for any specific instructions on items of clothing with sequins, beads, appliques, or fringe.

Delicate items that can get stretched or snagged by other items should be placed in a laundry net, and so should items with hardware that can catch and damage other items like bras.

Washing and Drying

Wash and dry according to the care instructions. Every washing machine and dryer is different, so you will have to figure out the dial setting for your desired cycle yourself. But generally, for each load, you put your clothes in the washing machine, add detergent, close the lid, set the dial for the proper water temperature and cycle, then push Start.

For clothing that cannot be placed in the dryer, you can either hang them to dry or lay them flat to dry. Again, follow the instructions. Knitwear or other stretchy material should be laid flat to dry on a rack or on a towel atop a table to avoid being stretched out of shape.

Clothing that sits right next to your skin, like underwear, should get washed after each wear. But things like sweaters that you wear over a shirt or undershirt, and even jeans and trousers don't always have to be washed each time. You can extend the life of these items by hanging them to air out between wears.

Removing Stains

A coffee spill on a favorite shirt, a ketchup blob on new jeans... Stains sure can ruin your day, but with the right approach, you can get rid of them like a wizard.

<u>The cardinal rule of stain removal:</u> Tackle it **ASAP**. As soon as you can, run to the bathroom and put some water on it. Put a little soap on the spot, and see if you can rub it off. Even if it doesn't completely go away, it's ok. You've delayed the stain from setting. Then — as soon as you can — spray stain remover on the spot (the type that you can apply and leave in the laundry basket till your next laundry day), and wash normally. Washing in hot water and drying without treating the stain can set it, so treat it first before throwing it in the wash.

There are some tough stains that require a little extra attention:

- **_Oil:_** Remove any oily solids from the fabric and soak up liquid oil with a paper towel. Use baking soda to pull even more oil out of the fabric. Apply a heavy-duty laundry detergent to the stained area, and see if it disappears.

- **_Blood:_** Turn the garment inside out and run _cold_ water from the inside to the outside. Scrub heavy-duty detergent into the stain with a soft-bristled brush or toothbrush. Let sit for 15 minutes, then launder as usual. <u>DO NOT use hot water on blood stains</u>, as it will set it permanently.

- For tougher stains, try a stronger stain remover.

Just remember, the faster you act, the better your chances.

Ironing

Ironing removes wrinkles and creases from your clothes, making you look sleek and even professional. So get your iron and ironing board out, and let's get to it.

Cotton and linen can handle high heat, while wool likes it medium. Delicate fabrics like silk or polyester prefer a cool setting. Always check the label on your clothes first and match the iron's dial setting accordingly. And if you're in doubt, start with a lower heat setting, then gradually turn up the temperature as needed.

Cotton and linen are also the only fabrics you should _dampen or use steam_ when ironing. If you put water in the iron to use the steam function, don't forget to dump it out after each use.

Otherwise, old water can stain your clothes the next time you use the iron.

By the way, the longer a piece of clothing is left wrinkled, the harder it is to get it out, so don't let your ironing pile up,

Storing Clothes

After all the effort you've put into washing, drying, and ironing, you want to make sure your clothes are stored properly, right?

For most clothes, folding or hanging should do the trick. T-shirts, sweaters, and jeans usually prefer to be folded, while dresses, blouses, and trousers like to hang. But watch out for overcrowded closets. Clothes need space to breathe, and squeezing them in too tightly can lead to wrinkles.

Delicate items like lingerie or beaded tops may need special care, like a separate drawer or a protective bag. Store your out-of-season clothes in a cool, dry place to keep them fresh for next year.

Clothes moths LOVE wool, cashmere, silk, and fur. The larvae of these pesky pests eat and leave little holes in your favorite sweaters and coats. So be sure to place moth repellents like cedarwood, lavender, or even mothballs where you store these items.

Clothes Moth --
Adult and Larva

MENDING AND ALTERING CLOTHES

Clothes are expensive. You can extend the life of your favorite clothing items by learning basic sewing and mending skills. Not only that, you can also take advantage of sales items or thrift store items that aren't quite right but can be easily altered to be a fabulous addition to your wardrobe.

If you don't already know how, it would be difficult to learn how to sew by reading a book like this. Sewing is a great skill to have, so find a way to learn it – watch YouTube videos, take a weekend class, or ask someone who knows how to teach you.

The most basic things you should strive to learn are:

1. Sewing on buttons and hooks

2. Shortening and lengthening straps

3. Raising and lowering a hem

4. Patching a hole or a tear

Taking care of your clothes isn't just about looking good; it's also about valuing what you have, reducing waste, and expressing your personal style.

BUILDING A BASIC WARDROBE

Your wardrobe is the portfolio of your style. It has to cover the basis, show your range, and be uniquely you.

Let's face it. You already know how to dress yourself: You know what kind of clothes you like, and you know how to make them look good. But as you gradually transition out of teendom into young adulthood, facing college/job interviews, internships, or full-time employment, the world is going to expect you to know how to dress differently.

Dressing for Different Occasions

Aim to build a wardrobe that has the following styles covered:

- **Casual:** This is your everyday attire. Think jeans, T-shirts, comfy shoes. It's all about comfort and expressing your personal style.

- **Business Casual:** Relaxed, yet polished. It's good for your work or a college interview. Women can opt for a dress, a skirt or dress pants paired with a blouse or a sweater; men can wear khakis or dress pants paired with a collared shirt.

A blazer can add a professional touch. Ties are optional (if you don't know how to tie a tie, hit YouTube straight away), and jackets can be worn but are not necessary. Shoes should still be formal. For winter, make sure you have at least one proper coat that goes well with business and formal attire.

- **Business Formal:** The most professional dress code. Men should wear a suit, a tie, and dress shoes. Women should opt for a business suit or a professional dress with conservative heels. This dress code is usually reserved for business meetings, conferences, or formal events.

- **Formal:** For weddings or black-tie events, a suit, a formal gown, or a cocktail dress is appropriate. Depending on the occasion, men might have to rent a tuxedo. Check the dress code for the occasion ahead of time.

- **Workout:** Invest in good quality activewear for your gym sessions or outdoor activities.

Dressing appropriately shows respect for the occasion and the people around you. You don't have to dress like everybody else; take it as a challenge to <u>flaunt your individuality while staying within conventional boundaries.</u>

Sustainable Fashion: Your Wardrobe, Your World

Dress to impress and stand for something more with sustainable fashion. When you choose sustainable fashion, you're not just nailing a look—you're choosing threads that respect the planet and your wallet, proving that style and smart choices go hand in hand. Wear your confidence as you make a positive impact, one outfit at a time.

- **Quality over Quantity:** Invest in well-made pieces that will last longer, rather than buying lots of cheap, low-quality items.

- **Secondhand Shopping:** Thrift stores, consignment shops, and online platforms offer pre-loved items at a fraction of the cost. And if you learn the basics of sewing, you can make simple alterations to slightly "off" items and expand your choices exponentially.

- *Care for Your Clothes:* Properly caring for your clothes extends their life. Repair items instead of replacing them.

- *Socially Conscious Brands:* Support brands that prioritize ethical labor practices and environmentally friendly processes.

Your wardrobe is not just a collection of clothes. It's an expression of who you are and what you value. Fashion is supposed to be fun, so don't be afraid to experiment, try new things, and let your personality shine through in your style!

Clothing care is an essential part of daily life that keeps you looking sharp and feeling confident. With a little effort in maintenance, you'll not only present yourself at your best but also save money and nurture a sense of independence. Besides, each garment cared for gets you closer to a polished and personalized style that's uniquely yours.

Chapter Eleven

Driving & Car Maintenance

Mastering the Ride

E veryone should <u>get a driver's license as soon as they can</u> — even if they don't own a car. Not only does it serve as a handy photo ID, but it also broadens your possibilities. The ability to drive gives you the freedom to rent a car for exciting road trips and access job opportunities that may otherwise be out of reach. Plus, as life gets busier in adulthood, finding the time to get your license becomes increasingly challenging. So **seize the opportunity now!**

YOUR DRIVER'S LICENSE

Getting Your License

In the United States, rules regarding driving lessons, learner's permits, and licenses vary by state, so be sure to check what they are where you live. But generally, the process usually follows a common pattern:

- *Learner's Permit*: Before you can begin official driving lessons or practice driving on public roads, many states require new drivers, especially teen drivers, to first obtain a *learner's permit*. (You'll probably have to take a test.) This permit typically allows you to drive only when accompanied by a licensed adult.

- *Driving Lessons*: Once you have a learner's permit, you can begin driving lessons. These lessons can be with a professional driving instructor or, in many cases, with a family member or friend who meets the state's requirements to supervise a new driver. Some states require a specific number of hours of supervised driving before a person can apply for a full driver's license.

- *Driver's Education:* In addition to hands-on driving lessons, many states also require new drivers, especially teens, to complete a driver's education course. This course covers the rules of the road, safe driving practices, and other essential knowledge. The course might include both classroom instruction and behind-the-wheel training. (Many suburban public high schools offer driving classes as part of their regular curriculum – including on-the-road driving lessons. If your school is one of them, take advantage of it while you can and save *a lot* of money.)

- *Full Driver's License:* After meeting all state requirements, including a specific period of holding a learner's permit, completing a certain number of supervised driving hours, and passing a road test, the individual can then obtain a full driver's license.

Renewing Your License

Your driver's license isn't something you get just once. Much like a library card or a gym membership, it needs to be renewed periodically. The renewal process varies by location, but it usually involves a visit to your local *DMV (Department of Motor Vehicles)* office to update your personal information, pass a vision test, and pay a renewal fee. Some places may require you to retake the written test, especially if you have let your license expire for a certain period of time.

SAFE DRIVING PRACTICES

You may be the best driver on the road – maybe you think you can handle anything, at any speed. **It doesn't matter.** The road is full of variables beyond your control – other drivers, pedestrians, kids, bicycles, animals, the weather, road conditions... the list goes on and on. So, let's go over the essentials of safe driving here.

- **Defensive Driving:** Drive like a chess player strategizing the next move; always thinking a step ahead, constantly alert, and ready to react promptly to any unforeseen move. Observe your surroundings, anticipate potential hazards, and respond appropriately. Keep a safe distance from the vehicle in front of you. Adjust your speed according to weather and traffic conditions, and always check your mirrors frequently to be aware of vehicles around you.

- **A good driver adapts their driving style** to the weather conditions. In *bad weather*, reduce your speed and increase the distance between you and the vehicle ahead. Use your wipers and headlights to improve visibility as well as to ensure others see *you*. In *foggy conditions*, use your *low-beam lights* for better visibility. If it's snowing or icy, drive slowly, brake gently, and be wary of *black ice*. In some states, *winter tires* are required for certain months of the year for extra safety.

- Recognize that when you are driving a car, you are moving a **serious piece of heavy machinery**, very fast. Let yourself be distracted for a fraction of a second – by your phone, a friend in the backseat, or someone on the side of the road – and you can cause some serious damage to yourself and others. Keep your attention focused on the road, your hands on the wheel, and your thoughts on the act of driving. <u>No text or call is worth a life</u>. If you need to use your phone or adjust your GPS, pull over safely before doing so.

BUYING A CAR

Buying a car may feel daunting, but if you need one or really, *really* want one, it can be done even on a teen's budget.

Step 1. Set Your Car Buying Budget: If you can spare $150 to $200 a month, you're on the right track. Decide on a realistic budget, consider your savings, earnings, and ways to cut expenses. Paying upfront can save on interest and open negotiation opportunities. For financing, seek help from someone with a credit history. Don't forget to consider costs of ownership like gas, maintenance, and insurance.

Step 2. Do Your Homework: Before car shopping, identify your needs. How will you use the car? How often will you drive? Any other drivers? List must-have features. Research online listings to find a fair price. Check safety, reliability, fuel efficiency, and more on sites like Cars.com, Edmunds, and Consumer Reports.

Step 3. Decide on a New or Used Car: Consider your budget when deciding between new and used. New cars offer low maintenance costs, advanced features, and warranties. Used cars are cost-effective, have lower insurance rates, and come in variety. Get a mechanic's opinion when buying a used one, if possible, to avoid surprises. Protect yourself; avoid too-good-to-be-true deals and check the car's history with the *VIN (Vehicle Identification Number)*.

Step 4. Take a Few Test Drives: Test drive to feel the car's performance. Inspect before driving, check the car's condition, and trust your senses. Review the car's features, read window stickers, and prepare for a half-hour drive. Test safety tech and ensure it suits your needs. Bring a trusted adult and get a pre-purchase inspection if needed.

Step 5. The Art of Negotiation: Negotiate the price; it's flexible. Research comparable prices, don't fall for add-ons, and be prepared to walk away if the deal isn't right. Review the entire contract, ask questions, and don't rush the paperwork. When buying used, research your state's rules for transferring ownership. Make sure you receive all car-related documents, and remember that once you agree to buy, it's final. Do your research ahead of time for the best value.

BASIC CAR MAINTENANCE AND REPAIR

Keeping your car in good condition by regularly performing basic maintenance and repairs can help enhance safety and save you a lot of money. These skills, however, are best learned by in-person hands-on training or watching instructional videos. It is much faster and safer that way. Below is a list of must-knows you should check off your list as soon as possible:

1. **Checking and Topping Up Fluids:** There are several fluids you need to pay attention to in a car, including *oil, coolant* (or anti-freeze), *transmission fluid* (if applicable), *brake fluid*, and *windshield washer fluid*.

2. **Changing a Flat Tire:** You just never know when you can get a flat on the road. You need to know how to use a *jack, spare tire*, and *lug wrench*, and know how to identify jacking points.

3. **Checking Tire Pressure:** You need to learn how to use a tire pressure gauge and inflate or deflate the tire to the proper air pressure. You can do this at the gas station.

4. **Replacing Windshield Wipers:** Got streaky windshields in bad weather? That can be dangerous. You know that, right? Watch YouTube on how to replace windshield wiper blades. It's SO simple!

5. **Changing the Air Filter:** Know how to locate the *air filter housing* and replace the filter.

6. **Jump-Starting a Car** when the battery runs down: How to use *jumper cables*, identify the positive and negative terminals, and connect to another vehicle's battery.

7. **Understanding Warning Lights:** Learn common dashboard warning lights, know their meanings, and know how to take appropriate actions. Some of these warnings can signal serious trouble, so don't take them lightly!

8. **Basic Troubleshooting:** Identifying common car problems, e.g., overheating and strange noises, and taking initial steps to diagnose issues, like checking for leaks.

9. **Regular Maintenance Schedule:** Understanding the manufacturer's recommended maintenance schedule and finding a trusted auto mechanic to perform the tasks.

Emergency Kit

There are certain items you should always have in your glove compartment or trunk in case of emergency. They are:

- **Flashlight** with **Extra Batteries, First-Aid Kit**, and **Blanket.**

- **Basic Tools:** Like screwdrivers, pliers, and an adjustable wrench.

- **Jumper Cables:** For reviving dead batteries.

- **Spare Tire, Jack, and Lug Wrench:** For changing a flat tire.

- **Reflective Triangles or Road Flares:** To alert other drivers if you're stopped on the road.

- **Weather Gear:** An ice scraper, windshield brush, and sand/kitty litter for traction in snow.

- **Bottled Water** and **Non-perishable Snacks:** In case you're stuck for a while.

CAR INSURANCE

Different Types of Insurance

Car insurance is the safety net that protects you from financial disasters that can result from road mishaps, but not all insurance is created equal. There are several types, each providing different levels of coverage.

You need to know this, so you can satisfy legal requirements.

- *Liability Insurance* is the <u>minimum legal requirement in most states</u>. It's your basic armor. It covers the costs if you're responsible for an accident and cause damage to another person's vehicle or property, or if you injure some-one.

- **Collision Insurance**, as the name suggests, covers damage to your own vehicle in an accident, whether you collide with another car or an object like a fence.

- **Comprehensive Insurance** covers damage to your car caused by events other than collisions, such as fire, theft, vandalism, or natural disasters.

- **Personal Injury Protection** and **Medical Payments Insurance** cover medical expenses for you and your passengers, regardless of who's at fault.

- **Uninsured and Underinsured Motorist Insurance** act as your backup, covering your costs if you're in an accident caused by a driver who doesn't have sufficient insurance or any at all.

It is often **illegal** to not have at least basic car insurance, but it is highly recommended to get as much insurance as you can afford to avoid huge bills in case you are involved in an accident.

Filing an Insurance Claim

If you're in an accident or something happens to your car, *filing a claim* is how you ask the insurance company to come to your rescue and cover the costs. After all, that's what you've been paying for!

The process starts with notifying your insurer about the incident. It's important to do this as soon as possible, *even if you're not at fault*. You'll need to provide details about the incident, including when and where it happened, who or what was involved, what damage was caused, and if there were any witnesses.

Next, a *claims adjuster* will investigate your claim. They piece together the evidence to figure out what happened and who's responsible. Once the investigation is complete, the insurance company will determine how much they will pay, based on the terms of your policy and the adjuster's findings. They'll then issue payment to you, the other party, or directly to the repair shop you use to fix your car.

Saving Money on Car Insurance

Car insurance is a must-have, but that doesn't mean it has to break the bank. There are several ways to smooth out the costs and make your policy more affordable.

- *Shop around:* Insurance rates can vary dramatically from one company to another. So, do your homework and compare quotes from different insurers.

- *Bundle up:* If you have other types of insurance, like homeowner's or renter's insurance, consider buying them from the same company. Many insurers offer discounts for bundling policies.

- *Maintain a clean driving record:* The fewer accidents and traffic violations you have, the lower your premium will be. This is where safe driving literally pays off!

- *Consider raising your deductible:* The higher your *deductible*, the lower your premium. But, of course, this means you'll pay more out of pocket if you have a claim, so you have to balance these factors.

- *Take advantage of discounts:* Many insurers offer discounts for things like completing a defensive driving course, installing a telematics device, or even being a good student.

- *Start on your parents' insurance policy:* This helps you build a driving record now so that you qualify for discounts on insurance later when you have to go independent.

WHAT TO DO IN CASE OF AN ACCIDENT

*Screeeech... **BANG!*** Okay, *now* what?

Safety First

The dust has barely settled, and your heart is still racing. You've just been in a car accident. It's a scary situation, but staying calm can help you navigate the aftermath more efficiently. First and foremost, <u>check yourself and others for any injuries</u>. If anyone is hurt, call for medical help immediately.

Next, call the police. Tell them you had an accident, and give them your location to the best of your abilities. The sooner you call the police, the better you will be protected from any unexpected situations that might follow.

If it's safe to do so, move your vehicle out of the traffic to a safe spot nearby. If that's not possible, turn on your hazard lights or set up safety triangles to warn other drivers of the accident. You need to <u>create a protective bubble around the accident scene</u> to prevent further mishaps.

Exchanging Information With the Other Driver

Once everyone's safe, it's time to exchange information with the other driver involved in the accident. (You will need this information to complete your insurance claim later.) Carefully get out of the car. You'll need to share your name, contact details, driver's license number, license plate number, and insurance information. Likewise, gather the same details from the other driver.

It's important to <u>stay calm and polite</u> during this interaction, even if the accident wasn't your fault. If the other driver refuses to share their information or attempts to leave the scene, take pictures of their license plate or write down the make and model of the vehicle along with any other details.

Documenting the Accident: Building Your Case

Next, document the accident. Take pictures of the accident scene, capturing the positions of the vehicles, any damage, road conditions, and any visible injuries. These photos can provide valuable proof when you're filing your insurance claim or if there's a dispute about who's at fault.

And before you forget, note down the details of the accident, including the date, time, location, and weather conditions. Jot down your account of how the accident happened while it's still fresh in your memory. Drawing a picture may feel funny, but it can help the police or your insurance company visualize the accident. This will serve as a reliable reference point in the future, especially if you need to recount the incident to your insurance company or the court.

Reporting the Accident to Insurance

Finally, report the accident to your insurance company so they can start the claims process. You can do this by calling your insurance agent or reporting it online or through your insurer's mobile app.

Provide as much detail as possible when reporting the accident. The information and photos you gathered at the scene will come in handy here. Be honest and thorough when describing the incident. Any discrepancies between your report and the official accident report can complicate the claims process.

Keep in mind, the sooner you report the accident, the better. Prompt reporting can speed up the claims process and get your vehicle back on the road sooner.

Car accidents can be stressful and disorienting, but knowing what steps to take in the aftermath can make the situation more manageable. Stay calm, prioritize safety, gather information, document the incident, and report it to your insurance company.

Driving and maintaining a car is much more than just a rite of passage; it's a responsibility that, when managed well, affords you independence and mobility. With the keys in hand and knowledge in mind, you're ready to navigate the roads ahead with confidence. Safe travels!

Chapter Twelve

Technology

Staying Smart in the Digital Age

Tech is your ticket to the world: for study, work, and staying in touch. But the online universe has its dangers—privacy invasions, scams, and risks that weren't even a "thing" when your parents were your age. Stay sharp, learn the ropes, and you'll be able to enjoy the internet's perks to the max while avoiding all the pitfalls.

PRIVACY AND SECURITY

Online Privacy and Security

Online privacy and security is like the lock on your front door, keeping your personal information safe from cyber intruders. When you're online, this lock is your password. It needs to be strong (a mix of letters, numbers, and symbols) and unique for each of your online accounts. Also, just as you wouldn't give your house keys to a stranger, don't share your passwords with anyone, even close friends.

Recognizing and Avoiding Scams

Scams fool you into seeing what's not there. They can come in various forms online: a suspicious email asking for your personal information, a pop-up warning that your computer is infected with a virus, or a too-good-to-be-true online deal. The key to avoiding scams is to *be skeptical*. Don't click on links from unknown sources, never share personal information with someone you don't trust, and when in doubt, do a quick online search to check if others have experienced a similar situation.

Cyberbullying Awareness and Prevention

Cyberbullying can be even more harmful than schoolyard bullying because it can happen anytime, anywhere, and can reach a vast audience. If you or someone you know is a victim of cyberbullying, don't stay silent. Report it to an adult, to the social media platform where it's happening, and to the police.

Laws are having a hard time keeping up in this area, but law enforcement is getting better at handling online crimes. Remember, everyone has the right to feel safe online, and each of us has a role in creating a respectful digital community.

Safe Social Media Practices

Social media is a wonderful way to share your joys in life with the world. But be warned: Once you post something online, it's almost impossible to take it back completely.

Think twice before sharing anything that you wouldn't want your future self, a college admissions officer, or a potential employer to see in the future. Be sure to adjust the privacy settings on your social media accounts to control who can see your posts and personal information.

Social media is a great way to meet new people and keep in touch with old friends, but it is also a way for scammers and criminals to learn more about you. Keep things like your school or work locations private, and don't post documents that contain information like an address, driver's license, or other personal identification.

The Impact of Digital Footprint

Every click, search, and "like" you post online is like a step in the digital sand, leaving a trail behind. These digital footprints paint a picture of your online behavior and preferences for others to see.

It's more than a record; it's a reflection of your virtual persona, tracing your journey across the web. Be aware that these virtual steps are not easily washed away by the tide of time. Think ahead and ensure your digital legacy is one you'll be proud to own.

Protecting Digital Identity

Your digital identity is a combination of all the personal information that exists about you online, such as your name, photos, and even your interests and opinions. Protecting your digital identity is crucial. Be aware of the information you're sharing online and with whom. Regularly check and update the privacy settings on your social media accounts, and be cautious when using public Wi-Fi, which can be less secure. Consider using a *VPN (Virtual Private Network)* in public spaces.

BASIC TROUBLESHOOTING

Restarting and Updating Devices: The Tech Refresh

Ever heard of the IT department's famous fix-all solution, "Have you tried **rebooting**?" It's a classic for a reason. Restarting your device can clear out the system's temporary data, stop running unnecessary applications, and fix many common issues. You are basically giving your device a little power nap to recharge and sort itself out.

Regular *updates* are like routine health check-ups for your devices. Updates often come with bug fixes, security patches, and new features. They make sure your device performs at its best, stays secure, and keeps up with the latest tech developments. So, next time you see that update notification, don't ignore it. Schedule it for a time when you're not using your device, and let it do its magic.

Dealing with Slow Internet

A slow internet connection can feel like you're stuck in a traffic jam while you're racing against time. Before you lose your cool, try these tips. First, <u>check your connection</u>. Are you connected to the right network? Could your device be too far from your Wi-Fi router? If your Wi-Fi signal is weak, moving closer to the router or using a wired connection can help.

If your connection is fine, the problem might be with your device. Close any unnecessary applications or browser tabs, as they can slow down your device and hog your bandwidth. If all else fails, give your router a restart. It's a simple trick that can often speed things up.

Managing Storage Space

Think of your device's storage space as a wardrobe. The more stuff you put in, the less room you have for new things. When your storage space starts to fill up, your device might slow down or not function properly. It's a sign that it's time for a digital clean-up.

Start by checking your storage settings to see what's taking up the most space. Is your gallery full of photos and videos? Or maybe it's that game you no longer play? Delete unnecessary files, uninstall unused apps, and move some of your stuff to the cloud.

DIGITAL LITERACY: Beyond Social Media

Using Search Engines Effectively

With so much information out there, knowing how to use search engines effectively is a key life skill. Start by crafting a precise search query. The more specific you are, the more relevant your results will be. Use keywords that directly relate to the information you're seeking. For example, instead of searching "weather," type "weather forecast New York City."

Learn to use *search operators* to refine your results. For instance, putting quotation marks around a phrase will search for that exact phrase. Using 'AND' in capital letters will ensure that both keywords are found in the search results, narrowing the number of results you get to more specific ones. On the other hand, using

'OR' in your query expands your options, as only one of the key-words needs to be found to return a result.

Finally, be sure to check multiple sources. Just because something appears at the top of the search results doesn't mean it's the most reliable source.

Evaluating Online Information

With vast amounts of information available online, it's like drown-ing in a sea of facts, opinions, and, unfortunately, misinformation. Therefore, knowing how to evaluate online information is more than important – it's vital.

Start by checking the source. Is it a reputable news outlet, aca-demic institution, or a recognized expert in the field? Or is it an anonymous blog post or social media comment?

Look at the date. In our fast-paced world, information can become outdated very quickly. Make sure the information is recent and still relevant. Also, cross-reference the information with other sources. If multiple credible sources present the same information, it's more likely to be accurate.

Basic Coding Skills

Imagine you're learning a new language that allows you to com-municate with computers. That's coding. Basic coding skills are becoming increasingly essential, not only for tech jobs but for a wide range of careers, including marketing & advertising, journal-ism, finance & banking, art & design, and medicine. It can be the difference between a mediocre and successful career.

You can start with an easy-to-learn language like Python or JavaScript. Plenty of free online resources, such as Codecade-my and Scratch, are designed to help beginners learn to code. Learning to code also helps improve problem-solving and logical thinking skills. It's like solving a puzzle or a riddle, where you must think step-by-step and consider different possibilities to reach the solution.

Digital Etiquette

Just like in real life, there are certain rules of behavior or etiquette we should follow when communicating online.

Be respectful of others' opinions, even if you disagree. It's possible to express your views without attacking or belittling someone else's. Remember that <u>tone can be hard to read online</u>. What you intend as a joke might come off as rude or offensive.

Be mindful of what you share. If it's not your news to share, or if it's something private or sensitive about someone else, it's better to stay quiet.

Remember <u>the golden rule of the internet</u>: Don't post anything you wouldn't want your grandma, your teacher, or your future employer to see. Because once it's out there, it's out there for good.

TECHNOLOGY FOR LEARNING AND PRODUCTIVITY

Online Learning Platforms: Your Virtual Classroom

Trade the four walls of your classroom for a limitless digital realm, ready to teach you anytime, anywhere. Welcome to the dynamic world of online learning platforms. From mastering a new language on Duolingo to learning to code on Codecademy, the possibilities are endless. You can follow a structured curriculum, learn at your own pace, and even earn certificates that can boost your resume. Plus, you get to learn from experts from all over the world, right from the comforts of your home. So, why wait? Pick a subject that piques your interest, and start expanding your knowledge today!

Productivity Apps: Your Digital Assistants

Think of productivity apps as your personal digital assistants, ready to lend a helping hand 24/7. Need to manage your tasks? Try apps that create to-do lists, set deadlines, and track progress.

Want to collaborate with others? Google Docs and Slack make teamwork a breeze. With the right productivity apps, you can stay organized, improve your focus, and work more efficiently. So, start exploring and find the apps that suit your needs best!

Digital Note-Taking

Swap out stacks of paper notebooks for one sleek digital platform. With digital note-taking, you can jot down ideas, sketch diagrams, embed images, and even capture audio all in one place. Apps like Evernote, Notion, or OneNote let you do all this and more. You can organize your notes into folders, tag them for easy search, and sync them across devices. Plus, you can share them with others for collaborative work. With digital note-taking, your notes are not only more organized but also more interactive and accessible.

Time Management Tools: Your Clock in the Cloud

Time management tools are like your virtual timekeepers, helping you make every second count. Need to break down your tasks into manageable intervals? Try the Pomodoro Technique with apps like TomatoTimer. Want to track how much time you spend on different tasks? There are apps out there that can give you a detailed breakdown.

Prefer to schedule your tasks on a calendar? Google Calendar or Outlook can sync your schedule across all your devices. By using time management tools, you can take control of your time, avoid procrastination, and boost productivity. So, start ticking those tasks off your list, one timely step at a time!

Keeping up with technology is not only about the gadgets and apps, but about how you use them to enhance your life. Embrace the digital age wisely, balancing the benefits of technology with the importance of real-world experiences. Stay curious, stay safe online, and never forget: technology is at its best when it helps you grow, connect, and achieve your goals.

Final Words

The journey to independence is just that — a journey.

As you venture forth on your own path to independence, two core principles will be your guiding stars: **resilience and adaptability**. Technology develops rapidly, and our world constantly evolves. So, while the skills you've gathered here provide a solid foundation, it's your resilience that will anchor you during tough times and your adaptability that will help you ride the waves of new opportunities and changes.

Embrace the challenges that come your way, learn from your mistakes, and continuously strive to grow. You've got the skills, the knowledge, and the determination to make your mark on the world. And hey, **you've got this book to refer back to** whenever you need it!

Here's to all the challenges you'll conquer, the skills you'll master, and the incredible journey you'll embark on! I can't wait to see where your journey takes you.

Ciao for now,

Love,

Trudy

References

Adolescents and STDs | Sexually Transmitted Diseases | CDC. (n.d.).
    https://www.cdc.gov/std/life-stages-populations/stdfact-teens.htm

Bankston, B. (2023, June 13). *Car buying guide for teens and new drivers*. Car
    Talk.
    https://www.cartalk.com/drivers-ed/car-buying-guide-for-teens-and-new-dr
    ivers

CHOC. (2023, June 23). *Social Media Tips for Kids and Teens - CHOC - Children's
    health hub*. CHOC - Children's Health Hub.
    https://health.choc.org/handout/social-media-tips-for-kids-and-teens/

Cleaning Supplies checklist | Molly Maid. (n.d.).
    https://www.mollymaid.com/cleaning-tips/schedules-charts-and-checklists/
    cleaning-supply-checklist/

CollegeData. (2022, November 22). How much does college cost? | CollegeData.
    CollegeData.
    https://www.collegedata.com/resources/pay-your-way/whats-the-price-tag-
    for-a-college-education

College prep: Teach your teenager how to do laundry. (n.d.). Dropps.
    https://www.dropps.com/blogs/spincycle/38213637-college-prep-teach-yo
    ur-teenager-how-to-do-laundry

Connection, R. (n.d.). Anxiety, stress, worry, and your body [medicinenet.com].
    PACEsConnection.
    https://www.pacesconnection.com/blog/anxiety-stress-worry-and-your-bod
    y-medicinenet-com

Contraception explained: Birth control options for teens & adolescents. (n.d.).
    HealthyChildren.org.
    https://www.healthychildren.org/English/ages-stages/teen/dating-sex/Pages
    /Birth-Control-for-Sexually-Active-Teens.aspx

Daily, L. (2022, December 2). *15 tools every homeowner should have. Washington
    Post.*
    https://www.washingtonpost.com/home/2022/05/24/essential-tools-homeo
    wners/

Drug Basics | Drug Overdose | CDC Injury Center. (n.d.).
    https://www.cdc.gov/drugoverdose/basics/index.html

Earn College Credit with CLEP – CLEP | College Board. (n.d.).
  https://clep.collegeboard.org/

Emotional Intelligence Handouts | Institute for Family Violence Studies. (n.d.).
  https://familyvio.csw.fsu.edu/clearinghouse-supervised-visitation/archive/e
  motional-intelligence-handouts

Fausett, R. (2021, August 6). *Five ways teens can use technology as a tool.* Troomi
  Wireless.
  https://troomi.com/five-ways-teens-can-use-technology-as-a-tool/

For Teens: How to make Healthy Decisions about sex. (n.d.). *HealthyChildren.org.*
  https://www.healthychildren.org/English/ages-stages/teen/dating-sex/Page
  s/Making-Healthy-Decisions-About-Sex.aspx

Get the Most Out of AP – AP Students | College Board. (n.d.).
  https://apstudents.collegeboard.org/

Hall, S. (2022, November 16). *How to Find a Good Roommate: 14 Steps (with
  Pictures) - wikiHow.* wikiHow.
  https://www.wikihow.com/Find-a-Good-Roommate

Harvard Health. (2021, February 15). *How to prevent infections.*
  https://www.health.harvard.edu/staying-healthy/how-to-prevent-infections#
  :~:text=Cover%20your%20mouth%20and%20nose,be%20examined%20b
  y%20a%20doctor.

Hay fever - Symptoms and causes - Mayo Clinic. (2022b, July 7). Mayo Clinic.
  https://www.mayoclinic.org/diseases-conditions/hay-fever/symptoms-caus
  es/syc-20373039

Healthy eating during adolescence. (2023, October 26). *Johns Hopkins Medicine.*
  https://www.hopkinsmedicine.org/health/wellness-and-prevention/healthy-
  eating-during-adolescence#:~:text=Eat%203%20meals%20a%20day,that
  %20are%20high%20in%20sugar.

Healthy eating plate. (2023c, January 31). The Nutrition Source.
  https://www.hsph.harvard.edu/nutritionsource/healthy-eating-plate/

The Human Condition. (2023, April 30). *Automatic negative thoughts: what they
  are, causes, and how to overcome them.*
  https://thehumancondition.com/automatic-negative-thoughts/

I'm Pregnant, Now What? | Pregnancy Options For Teens. (n.d.). Planned
  Parenthood.
  https://www.plannedparenthood.org/learn/teens/stds-birth-control-pregnan
  cy/i-think-im-pregnant-now-what#:~:text=If%20your%20pregnancy%20te
  st%20is,to%20do%20about%20your%20pregnancy.

In-Network vs. Out-of-Network Providers | Cigna. (n.d.).
  https://www.cigna.com/knowledge-center/in-network-vs-out-of-network#:~
  :text=Plans%20may%20vary%2C%20but%20in,live%2C%20network%20
  availability%20may%20vary.

Insurance and billing | Boston Medical Center. (n.d.). *Boston Medical Center.*
  https://www.bmc.org/stroke-and-cerebrovascular-center/patient-informatio
  n/insurance-and-billing

Interview tips for Teens. (n.d.).
    https://www.bgca.org/news-stories/2021/June/interview-tips-for-teens
*Jkennedy. (2023, June 22). Helpful vs. Harmful Ways to Manage Emotions. Mental
    Health America.
    https://screening.mhanational.org/content/helpful-vs-harmful-ways-manag
    e-emotions/*
Lake, R. (2023, October 3). Best savings accounts for kids for October 2023 ·
    TIME stamped. *TIME Stamped.*
    https://time.com/personal-finance/article/best-savings-accounts-for-kids/
Loh, A. (2021, February 3). 15 Must-Have Kitchen Tools. *EatingWell.*
    https://www.eatingwell.com/article/50233/must-have-kitchen-tools/
Martin, A. (2023, August 6). *Coinsurance vs. Copays: What's the Difference?*
    Investopedia.
    https://www.investopedia.com/articles/insurance/120816/coinsurance-vs-c
    opay-why-you-need-know-difference.asp#:~:text=A%20copay%20is%20a
    %20set,you've%20met%20your%20deductible.
McGuire, V. C., & Lambarena, M. (2023, June 1). *Student Credit Cards 101:
    Everything you need to know.* NerdWallet.
    https://www.nerdwallet.com/article/credit-cards/student-credit-cards-101
Miller, C., & Taskiran, S., MD. (2023, October 30). *Mental health disorders and
    teen substance use.* Child Mind Institute.
    https://childmind.org/article/mental-health-disorders-and-substance-use/
Movement, Q.-. P. a. P. W. (2023, January 2). Is Inflation High Compared To Years
    Past? Breaking Down Inflation Rates By Year. *Forbes.*
    https://www.forbes.com/sites/qai/2023/01/02/is-inflation-high-compared-to
    -years-past-breaking-down-inflation-rates-by-year/?sh=27d684b16d7a
MyDoh. (2022b, September 19). *Insurance 101: A Guide for parents and Teens |
    MyDoh.* Mydoh.
    https://www.mydoh.ca/learn/money-101/insurance/insurance-101-a-guide-
    for-parents-and-teens/
*Nivea. (2023, August 2). Teenage skin care tips. Skin Care | NIVEA.
    https://www.nivea.co.uk/advice/skin/teenage-skin-care-tips*
Physical activity guidelines for Americans | Health.gov. (n.d.).
    https://health.gov/our-work/nutrition-physical-activity/physical-activity-gu
    idelines
Pomroy, K. (2022, August 6). *Should I use a guarantor or cosigner on a rental
    agreement?*
    https://www.experian.com/blogs/ask-experian/guarantor-vs-cosigner/
Robinson, D. (2023, October 12). *Cheapest car insurance for teens.* MarketWatch.
    https://www.marketwatch.com/guides/insurance-services/teenage-drivers-i
    nsurance/
Ross, K. M., & Moody, J. (2020, April 7). 10 ways to help your teen with the
    college decision. *US News & World Report.*
    https://www.usnews.com/education/best-colleges/slideshows/parents-10-w
    ays-to-help-your-teen-with-the-college-decision

SAMHSA's national helpline. (n.d.). SAMHSA.
   https://www.samhsa.gov/find-help/national-helpline
The simple guide to health plans. (n.d.-b). Aetna.
   https://www.aetna.com/health-guide/hmo-pos-ppo-hdhp-whats-the-differen
   ce.html
Sulpy, E., & Adkins, C. (2022, December 8). *How to teach basic car maintenance
   to your teen | GetJerry.com.*
   https://getjerry.com/advice/how-to-teach-basic-car-maintenance-to-your-te
   en-by-elaine-sulpy
Surgeon, R. R. E. H. a. N. (2022, April 7). *What is an emotional trigger?*
   MedicineNet.
   https://www.medicinenet.com/what_is_an_emotional_trigger/article.htm
Take charge of your health: a guide for teenagers. (2023, September 22). National
   Institute of Diabetes and Digestive and Kidney Diseases.
   https://www.niddk.nih.gov/health-information/weight-management/take-ch
   arge-health-guide-teenagers
Teens and social media use: What's the impact? (2022, February 26). Mayo Clinic.
   https://www.mayoclinic.org/healthy-lifestyle/tween-and-teen-health/in-dep
   th/teens-and-social-media-use/art-20474437#:~:text=Because%20of%20te
   ens'%20impulsive%20natures,bullied%2C%20harassed%20or%20even%2
   0blackmailed.
Teens: hygiene & dental care. (2020, January 1). *Raising Children Network.*
   https://raisingchildren.net.au/teens/healthy-lifestyle/hygiene-dental-care
Teens taking charge of their health. (2020, March 2). *NIH News in Health.*
   https://newsinhealth.nih.gov/2020/02/teens-taking-charge-their-health
The simple guide to health plans. (n.d.-b). Aetna.
   https://www.aetna.com/health-guide/hmo-pos-ppo-hdhp-whats-the-differen
   ce.html
What is a 529 plan? - Savingforcollege.com. (2023, October 27).
   Savingforcollege.com.
   https://www.savingforcollege.com/intro-to-529s/what-is-a-529-plan#:~:tex
   t=A%20529%20college%20savings%20plan,for%20qualified%20higher%
   20education%20expenses.
Whitbourne, K. (2018, January 19). *What are the different types of doctors?*
   WebMD.
   https://www.webmd.com/health-insurance/insurance-doctor-types
wikiHow. (2023, July 5). *How to Buy Vegetables: 6 Steps (with Pictures) - wikiHow.*
   wikiHow. https://www.wikihow.com/Buy-Vegetables
World Health Organization: WHO. (2022, October 5). Physical activity.
   https://www.who.int/news-room/fact-sheets/detail/physical-activity
Zutobi. (2023, May 3). *Starting to Drive as a Teen 101 – Learn How To
   Drive a Car. Zutobi Drivers Ed.*
   https://zutobi.com/us/driver-guides/learning-how-to-drive
24-Hour movement guidelines – Canadian 24-Hour movement guidelines. (n.d.).
   https://csepguidelines.ca/

Your Review Can Make a Difference!

Hi There! I really hope you enjoyed this book.

Are you feeling a little more confident and prepared now to tackle the real-life challenges ahead of you?

Do you think there may be other teens and young adults out there who may benefit from this book, too?

If so, please take 60 seconds to leave a review. It's super easy!

1. Scan the code above. It'll take you directly to the review page.

2. Leave a star rating, and if you are so inclined...

3. Say a few words about how this book may have helped you.

Who knows? That may be the thing that convinces someone to choose this book — which will change their life for the better!

BTW, if you would like to order another copy or a print version of this book, just click the link below:

Thank you from the bottom of my heart!

Love, Trudy

Made in the USA
Las Vegas, NV
24 November 2024